A Journey into Mohawk and Oneida Country,

1634–1635

The Journal of Harmen Meyndertsz van den Bogaert

Translated and Edited by
Charles T. Gehring
and
William A. Starna

Wordlist and Linguistic Notes by
Gunther Michelson

SYRACUSE UNIVERSITY PRESS

First Paperback Edition 1991
98 99   6 5 4 3 2

This book is published with the assistance of a grant from the John Ben Snow
Foundation.

The paper used in this publication meets the minimum requirements of American National Standard for Information Sciences—Permanence of Paper for
Printed Library Materials, ANSI Z39.48-1984. ∞™

Library of Congress Cataloging-in-Publication Data

Bogaert, Harmen Meyndertsz van den.
    A journey into Mohawk and Oneida country, 1634–1635 : the journal
of Harmen Meyndertsz van den Bogaert / translated and edited by
Charles T. Gehring and William A. Starna : wordlist and linguistic
notes by Gunther Michelson. — 1st paperback ed.
    p. cm. — (The Iroquois and their neighbors)
    Translation from the Dutch.
    Includes bibliographical references.
    ISBN 0-8156-2546-4
    1. New York (State)—Description and Travel. 2. Bogaert, Harmen
Meyndertsz van den—Journeys—New York (State) 3. Dutch—Travel—
New York (State)—History—17th century. 4. Dutch—New York
(State)—History—17th century. 5. Mohawk River Region (N.Y.)—
Description and travel. I. Gehring, Charles T., 1939–
II. Starna, William A. III. Title. IV. Series.
F122.1.B6 1991
917.4704′2—dc20   91-2897
                                                            CIP

MANUFACTURED IN THE UNITED STATES OF AMERICA

A Journey into Mohawk and Oneida Country, 1634–1635 5/23

3-

THE
Iroquois
AND THEIR
NEIGHBORS

Laurence M. Hauptman, Series Editor

Fig. 1. *Fort Orange, 1635,* © 1986 by Leonard F. Tantillo.
Reprinted by permission of Leonard F. Tantillo.

This volume is respectfully dedicated to
WILLIAM N. FENTON,
Distinguished Professor of Anthropology Emeritus,
Dean of Iroquoianists, teacher, scholar, and trusted friend.

CHARLES T. GEHRING was born in Fort Plain, New York, in the heart of the Mohawk Valley. He has a Ph.D. in Germanic Linguistics from Indiana University with a concentration in Netherlandic Studies. His dissertation (1973) was a linguistic investigation of the survival of the Dutch language in colonial New York. He is presently director of the New York State Library's New Netherland Project, which is responsible for translating the official records of the Dutch colony and promoting awareness of the Dutch role in American colonial history.

WILLIAM A. STARNA is a native of the Middle Mohawk Valley, having grown up in St. Johnsville. He received his Ph.D. in Anthropology from the State University of New York at Albany in 1976, and is a long-time student of Iroquoian and Algonquian Indian populations in the Eastern Woodlands. His teaching and research interests include ethnohistory, prehistory, and applied anthropology, and he has held a Senior Fellowship at the Nelson A. Rockefeller Institute of Government. He is presently Professor and Chairman of the Department of Anthropology, State University of New York, College at Oneonta.

GUNTHER MICHELSON is an Iroquoian linguist residing in Montreal.

Contents

PREFACE

ᴇɴᴅʀɪᴄᴋ Hᴜᴅꜱᴏɴ's historic voyage of 1609 to the New World was soon followed by a steady flow of traders from the Netherlands. It was only a matter of time before expeditions were sent into the interior to seek out precious metals or to treat with the Indians.

The first record of any Dutch exploration appears on an early map of New Netherland. The passage reports how in 1614 a trader named Kleyntjen traveled westward into the interior, then southward from the *Maquas* (Mohawks) along the New River (Susquehanna) to the *Ogehage* (Mohawk name for the Minquas or Susquehannocks). Although it is sparse information, it does represent the earliest account of Dutch explorations west of the Hudson River. If Kleyntjen kept a journal or wrote a report of his adventure, it has been lost. If other traders or employees of the West India Company ventured westward after Kleyntjen, their reports and accounts have also been lost, or disposed of in the great archival housecleaning of 1674, when the Company was reorganized.

It is ironic that the first detailed account of the Dutch in Iroquois country survived only because a copy of it fell into private hands. Without the Harmen Meyndertsz van den Bogaert journal, we would be deprived of the earliest known description of the Lower Iroquois and their environment, including detailed accounts of their settlements, healing rituals, systems of protocol, language, and subsistence practices. It stands as a unique and compelling document.

A translation of this type is inevitably indebted to many people and institutions. First and foremost we extend our gratitude to William N. Fenton, to whom this volume is dedicated. It was he who first introduced us to the journal and its value as a historic document many years ago. And it was he who encouraged us to complete the new translation and to produce the endnotes. This took more than the form of pats on the back. In 1976, he facilitated a request for a travel grant to the Huntington Library in San Marino, California, to examine the original document. In addition, he has listened to several papers we have presented on the journal, has discussed its contents with us, and read our manuscript in draft form. Throughout, he has remained steadfast in his support and continued patience with our efforts.

We wish to thank Jack Campisi, Robert E. Funk, George Hamell, and Elisabeth Tooker, who read the manuscript in its several draft forms, offering helpful criticisms and suggestions.

We are also indebted to the Trustees of the Henry E. Huntington Library and Art Gallery for the research grant that made it possible to study the Van den Bogaert journal in its manuscript form.

A special note of appreciation goes to Leonard F. Tantillo of Schodack, New York, for allowing us to reproduce his painting *Fort Orange, 1635*, in this work.

The map was drawn by Ronald E. Embling, Instructional Resource Center, State University of New York, College at Oneonta. A facsimile page of the original document was prepared by Charles D. Winters, also of SUNY Oneonta. It is reproduced with the kind permission of the Huntington Library. In addition, Winters prepared the several plates found in our volume.

Finally, we would like to thank Ann Pasternak and Nancy A. M. Zeller for their assistance in preparing the manuscript.

The linguistic material contained in the endnotes was provided by Gunther Michelson of Montreal, Quebec, Canada. He also authored the Mohawk language wordlist and translations which follow the text of the journal and endnotes. His expert analysis of the language in the Indian passages and wordlist provides a new and important dimension to the journal which was lacking in any of the previous translations. We are grateful for his participation in this project and patient cooperation in the final production of this work. He is the best of colleagues, and we value his skills and friendship.

INTRODUCTION

In 1621, the Dutch West India Company (WIC) was chartered by the States General of the United Provinces of the Netherlands. Its primary objective was to carry on the war with Spain in the Atlantic region after the expiration of the Twelve Years' Truce. The truce had been agreed upon in 1609, after forty-one years of rebellion against the Habsburg Empire. This short interval, in what was to become known as the Eighty Years' War for Independence, was used by the Dutch to develop new markets throughout the world and to explore for new and more economical trade routes. Earlier, the Dutch East India Company, chartered in 1602, undertook a venture that had resulted in the United Provinces' claim to a huge expanse of territory in North America between New England and the English colonies on the Chesapeake. In 1609, when Hendrick Hudson sailed up the river now bearing his name, he was hoping to find a shorter and safer route to the Spice Islands in the Far East. Instead, he happened upon the most natural access to the interior of North America and its riches south of New France. The importance of Hudson's discovery was soon realized by merchants in the Netherlands who petitioned the States General for licenses to exploit the resources of the New World.

The natural resource which drew these merchants to the coast of America was the beaver. Current fashion in Europe

Fig. 2. Pieter Goos's chart, with coat of arms (1666), from
*Paskaerte van de Zuydt en Noordt Revier in Nieu Nederlandt
Strechende van Capo Hinloopen tot Rechkewach* [*"Vignette"*].

required a steady flow of pelts for the hat-making industry.
According to preliminary explorations, there was every indi-
cation of an unlimited supply of this furbearing animal in what
was soon to be called *Nieuw Nederlant* (New Netherland). The
situation was perfect for any merchant interested in making a
profit. The navigable North and South rivers (Hudson and
Delaware, respectively) afforded easy access to the interior,
where trading posts could be established, while the natives, who
were eager for European material goods, could bring their furs
to the trading posts with a minimal amount of effort expended

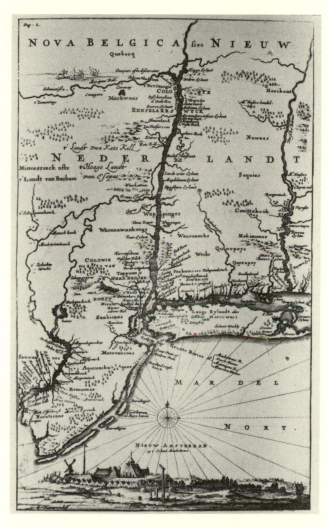

Fig. 3. *Nova Belgica sive Nieuw Nederlandt* [insert view] *Nieuw Amsterdam op t Eylant Manhattans* [The Van der Donck Map and View], 1651–1655, from *Beschryvinge Van Nieuw-Nederlandt.*

on the merchants' part. Thus, in 1621, when the West India Company was chartered, it was also given a monopoly of the fur trade in New Netherland. A network had already been established by private traders during the truce years. Now it was only necessary for the Company to refine the manner of collection and to protect its interests.

The WIC was organized along the lines of the successful East India Company. As a stock operation with shareholders both large and small, its charter gave it the power to declare war on and to conclude treaties with the natives in its area of economic jurisdiction from the west coast of Africa to the mid-Pacific. The Company had its own army and navy and was expected to make profits by capturing Spanish ships and capitalizing on the natural resources of its territories. Its governing body was known as the XIX, symbolizing the nineteen directors who came from various regions of the United Provinces. The provinces of Holland and Zeeland held a controlling majority in the company, with representation by eight and six directors, respectively. Holland's interest was represented by the "chamber" at Amsterdam, which was responsible for the administration of affairs in New Netherland.

In 1624, the Amsterdam chamber of the Company established trading posts on the three rivers which led into the interior of its territory in North America: on High Island (now Burlington Island, in New Jersey) in the Delaware River, at Fort Orange (Albany, New York) on the west bank of the Hudson River, and at Fort Hope (Hartford, Connecticut) along the Connecticut River. At this time thirty-two families were sent over to form agricultural communities near these posts as support for the fur-trading operations.

The first director, Willem Verhulst, arrived in the colony in 1625, with instructions to establish his administrative center on High Island because of the mistaken notion that its southern location would offer it a climate conducive to year-round accessibility. He was also instructed to avoid any involvement in local Indian disputes. In 1626, however, Verhulst's commander at Fort Orange, Daniel van Crieckenbeeck, ignored this policy by siding with the Mahican in a war against the Mohawk. The disasterous defeat of the Mahican at the hands of their arch-enemy, including the death of the Dutch commander and several of his soldiers, led to a dangerous situation at the three fur-trading posts. The Mohawk, heavily outnumbering the Dutch, were in a position to take retaliatory measures by destroying the small communities in these remote areas, delivering a setback to Company operations from which it might not recover.

This critical state of affairs was resolved by the new director, Peter Minuit, who replaced Verhulst in the spring of the same year, after the latter had fallen into disfavor and was recalled to the Netherlands. In order to insure the safety of the settlers, Minuit withdrew all the families to the recently purchased Manhattan Island, where they were to establish support farms for the Company's new center of operations.

Fort Orange and the other posts were maintained by a handful of soldiers while negotiations were carried on with the Mohawk. The Dutch apparently were able to assure the Mohawk that the actions against them were the decision of a local commander acting against orders. The Dutch negotiators, led by Pieter Barentsz, were not only able to pacify this Iroquois group, thus preventing retaliatory strikes against their vulnerable posts, but they also managed to establish a bond of mutual interest and friendship which was never broken. Dutch dependency on the Mohawk became so strong that in later years they were called upon to mediate Indian disputes as far away as the South River region of New Netherland and they served as enforcers of Dutch interests against other Indian tribes. The proximity of the Mohawk to Fort Orange also discouraged potential enemies, such as the French to the north and New

Englanders to the east, from raiding this area, which was more than 100 miles upriver from Manhattan and cut off from any relief during the winter months.

It was almost five years after the Crieckenbeeck disaster before any serious attempt was made to resettle the area around Fort Orange. Rather than assume the added burden of colonization, the WIC yielded to the pressures of a faction of the directors who were in favor of promoting agricultural settlements in New Netherland by means of privately financed ventures called patroonships. Under this system, permitted by a concession to the WIC charter called the "Freedoms and Exemptions," WIC directors were allowed to negotiate with the natives for a specified amount of land on the condition that they send more than fifty settlers to that area within four years and not become involved in the fur trade.

Patroonships were established from the Connecticut River to Delaware Bay; however, the only one which managed to survive was Rensselaerswyck, in which Kiliaen van Rensselaer, an Amsterdam diamond merchant and WIC director, had a controlling interest. His colony eventually contained almost one million acres of land (approximately present-day Albany and Rensselaer counties) on both sides of the Hudson River, with the WIC trading post of Fort Orange situated almost in its geographical center. The patroonship had its own court system and government but was ultimately responsible to the WIC. Capital crimes, for example, could be appealed to the court in New Amsterdam. During the administrations of the WIC directors Wouter van Twiller and Willem Kieft, Fort Orange and Rensselaerswyck were dependent on one another for survival, with the patroonship furnishing agricultural support to the Company's fur-trading operation and the fort providing security for the colonists of Rensselaerswyck. By 1653, the Fort Orange/Rensselaerswyck region claimed to have 230 men capable of bearing arms.

Since the Dutch first began exploiting this area, they had been in direct contact with the French fur-trading operations in New France along the St. Lawrence River. The Dutch had been trading with and supporting the Mohawk, who controlled the major trading route through the Mohawk Valley. The French, on the other hand, had a strong alliance with the Huron, who were constantly in conflict with the Mohawk over the control of fur-trapping regions. French attempts to gain control of the fur trade to the west around Oneida Lake were a major concern of the Dutch. If the French were allowed to negotiate a truce with the Iroquois and to establish a trading operation at Oneida, the Dutch fur-trading post at Fort Orange would become an anachronism and New Netherland would cease to be a profitable and viable investment for the WIC. It is in this context that Harmen Meyndertsz van den Bogaert was called upon to lead an expedition into Iroquois country.

In the winter of 1634, the commissary of Fort Orange, Marten Gerritsen, sent a party of three WIC employees into the Iroquois country. Their mission was to investigate the decline in the fur trade, possibly caused by French incursions, and to negotiate a new price structure for the furs. The expedition consisted of Harmen Meyndertsz van den Bogaert, Jeronimus dela Croix, and Willem Thomassen. Unfortunately, only the latter two men are mentioned by name in the journal. When the journal was first made public in 1895, its authorship was attributed to one Arent van Curler, an employee of Rensselaerswyck. Nonetheless, it was later pointed out by A. J. F. van Laer, the archivist at the New York State Library, that Van Curler had not arrived in the colony until 1638. Van Laer suggested instead, that Van den Bogaert was the leader of the party and author of the journal. He based this on the fact that Van den Bogaert was employed as barber-surgeon at Fort Orange during the 1630s. The journal itself implies that the author

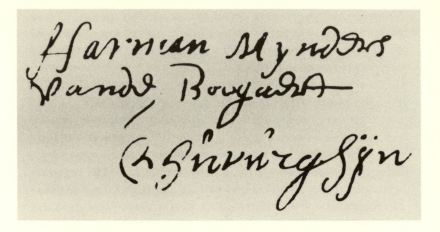

Fig. 4. The signature of Harmen Meyndertsz van den Bogaert, Surgeon, from *The History of New Netherland* by E. B. O'Callaghan (D. Appleton and Co., New York, 1855).

was a surgeon because, on December 21, 1634, he was called upon to cure a sick Indian. He also exhibited an interest in Indian healing ceremonies. In addition to this, twelve years later Van den Bogaert sought refuge in Iroquois country to avoid prosecution. It is not improbable that someone unfamiliar with the Mohawk Valley would have chosen to flee there; however, it does strengthen the case for presuming Van den Bogaert's authorship if we assume that he was escaping to a familiar territory.

On May 24, 1630, the eighteen-year-old barber-surgeon arrived in New Netherland aboard the West India Company ship *De Eendracht*. There are no records of his early duties in the colony, although we presume that he was posted to Fort Orange as Company surgeon soon after his arrival. His name first appears in the "Dutch Colonial Manuscripts" in 1638, where he gives his age as twenty-six and profession as surgeon. Thus, Van den Bogaert would have been only twenty-three years old when he led the expedition into Iroquois country. In 1640, he married Jelisje Claesen, by whom he had four children. Besides his medical duties, Van den Bogaert became involved in other activities at Fort Orange, beginning in 1634 with his mission to the Iroquois. Four years later he became part owner of the privateer *La Garce,* which he sailed to the West Indies for the purpose of taking Spanish prizes. Upon his return to the colony in 1640, he was appointed commissary of stores on Manhattan. It was probably the experience gained in this office, in addition to his familiarity with the upper Hudson region, that led to his appointment as commissary at Fort Orange in 1645.

Van den Bogaert's career, however, took a sudden turn in the fall of 1647, when he fled into the Mohawk Valley to avoid prosecution on a charge of sodomy committed with his black servant Tobias. Five days after entering Indian country, his servant was seized, but Van den Bogaert managed to avoid capture and find refuge among the same people he had visited thirteen years before. It was sometime during the winter that Hans Vos, an employee of Rensselaerswyck, was sent out to capture the fugitive. Vos cornered Van den Bogaert in an Indian storehouse, which burned to the ground in the confrontation. Van den Bogaert was captured and returned to Fort Orange to await the resolution of his case.

The whole affair was considered so important that an Indian messenger was sent overland to New Amsterdam in order to inform the new director, Petrus Stuyvesant, of these events. Stuyvesant, after receiving a complaint from the Indians regarding their losses in the fire, decided in council to compensate them by selling Van den Bogaert's garden plot on Manhattan and giving them the proceeds. He then delayed final resolution of the case until further information could be secured from Fort Orange in the spring. However, before the communication link could be reestablished with Fort Orange by ship, Van den Bogaert escaped imprisonment. As he ran over the frozen river to avoid recapture by soldiers from the fort, the ice broke underneath him and he was drowned.

The other two members of the party had less tumultuous careers. Willem Thomassen eventually became master of the private ship *De Valckenier* which, ironically, probably brought the news of Van den Bogaert's death to New Amsterdam. Jeronimus dela Croix returned to the Netherlands a few years after the expedition into Iroquois country, bringing with him this copy of Van den Bogaert's journal for Kiliaen van Rensselaer.

The journal is made up of rag paper leaves measuring 14 × 12⅛ inches or 47 cm. × 37 cm. Each leaf is folded in half to form four pages; nine leaves are sewn together with white thread to form a total of thirty-six pages, thirty-two of which contain the journal entries and a Mohawk-Dutch vocabulary. The paper itself contains a watermark identified as the "Arms of Baden Hochberg," which establishes it as Rhenish paper. The first page, which serves as the front cover, carries the identifying mark "No. R." This follows the Dutch record-keeping system of using alphabetical letters as reference marks; when single letters were exhausted, they were then doubled and tripled, etc.

The handwriting is clear and shows the careful execution of a clerk or secretary trained in recording and copying records. Errors in the text indicate that it was copied from Van den Bogaert's original. In several instances it is obvious that the copyist was uncertain of the handwriting he was transcribing. At times, the context made it clear that he was in error and he corrected himself. At other times the errors were retained. Such scribal errors would not have been made by the person who kept the original. We assume, therefore, that shortly after Van den Bogaert's return to Fort Orange a copy was made at the request of officials in Rensselaerswyck. Although Kiliaen van Rensselaer was prohibited at this time by the "Freedoms and Exemptions" from engaging in the fur trade, he did monitor it carefully and would have been extremely interested in the negotiations with the Iroquois because any incursions by the French in the fur trade would have had a direct impact on his possessions along the Hudson. We believe that the journal was copied by an official of Rensselaerswyck and sent to the patroon in Amsterdam for his own information. It may also be possible that the journal was copied by Jeronimus dela Croix with the intention of submitting it to Kiliaen van Rensselaer when he returned to the Netherlands. In 1638, Kiliaen van Rensselaer wrote to Wouter van Twiller that "Ieronimus La Croix has also communicated to me the circumstances of his journeys through the maquans land to the Sinnekens" (Van Laer 1980, p. 401). There it remained among Van Rensselaer's papers until 1895, when it was discovered and purchased by General James Grant Wilson. The original was probably among the papers of the West India Company archives in Amsterdam which were disposed of in 1674 when the Company was reorganized.

The disposition of the manuscript and its ultimate acquisition by the Henry E. Huntington Library in San Marino, California, is an interesting account in itself. Wilson (1895, 1896) states that the journal was discovered and obtained by him in the summer of 1895 while in Holland, and was subsequently translated and published. J. Franklin Jameson (1909, p. 137), acknowledging Wilson's discovery, claimed that it was identical to a journal mentioned by Nicolaas de Roever, the late archivist of the city of Amsterdam, in his articles in *Oud Holland* on Kiliaen van Rensselaer, appearing in the *Van Rensselaer Bowier Manuscripts*.

General James Grant Wilson (1832–1914) was born in Edinburgh, Scotland. One year later, his family emigrated to the United States, taking up residence in Poughkeepsie, New York. Following his education, Wilson moved to Chicago, where he edited and published a number of periodicals. In 1862, he was commissioned an officer in the 15th Illinois Cavalry and later the 4th United States Colored Cavalry, seeing action in several campaigns in the Mississippi Valley. He resigned his commission in 1865, living the remainder of his life in New York City. His writings were prolific, consisting mainly of biographies, and he was a member of many professional organizations including the American Ethnological Society (President, 1900–1914), and the American Authors' Guild (President, 1892–1899).

Following the initial publication of the journal in *The Independent* (1895), and later for the American Historical Association (1896), Wilson appears to have sold the original manuscript. William M. Beauchamp (1830–1925), an early student of the Iroquois, mentions in a letter to Samuel L. Frey (1833–1924), a historian of the Mohawk Valley, the fact that by 1908 Wilson no longer had the journal but only the translation he had made (Frey n.d.). Also corresponding with Frey was Myron F. Westover, a past president of the Schenectady Historical Society. He informed Frey that the journal had been purchased by a "Mr. White" for $800 (Frey n.d.), a considerable sum at the time. Apparently, Westover was first told of the existence of the manuscript by Dr. William Elliott Griffis (1843–1928), a former pastor of the First Reformed Church in Schenectady, New York, who also indicated that the owner was a "Mr. White" from Brooklyn. "Mr. White" was William Augustus White (1843–1927), a wealthy manufacturer, bibliophile, and collector, and a close friend of a vice-president of General Electric, headquartered in Schenectady. At Westover's request, he brought the journal to Schenectady, where it was shown to A. J. F. van Laer (1869–1955), the previously mentioned archivist and translator of Dutch (Frey n.d.). The fact of White's ownership is further strengthened by the presence of the initials "W. A. W." pencilled in the lower right corner of the otherwise blank verso of the title page of the journal.

Sometime after 1908, Henry E. Huntington (1850–1927), the railroad executive and financier, procured the original manuscript. Today it is in the collections of his library in San Marino, California, cataloged as HM 819. There are no acquisition records regarding the journal, nor is there any other information as to how it was obtained. A library official suspects that it was acquired during Huntington's lifetime, when record-keeping on the provenience of manuscripts was sometimes less than adequate.

To the best of our knowledge, Wilson's translation of the manuscript is the first. A revision appears in Jameson's (1909, pp. 135–62) volume, completed by S.G. Nissensen from the original. Ours is the third.

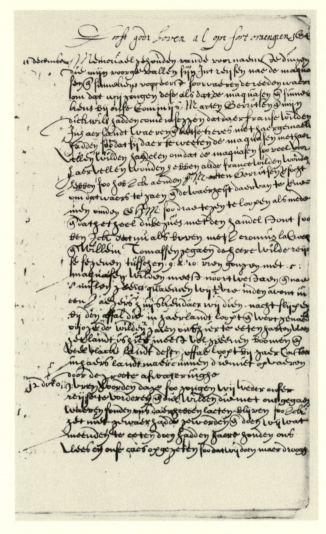

Fig. 5. The first page of Van den Bogaert's journal. Courtesy of the Henry E. Huntington Library and Art Gallery, San Marino, California.

THE JOURNAL OF
HARMEN MEYNDERTSZ VAN DEN BOGAERT

Praise God above all. At Fort Orange 1634.

11 December. Report of the most important things that happened to me while traveling to the Maquasen and Sinnekens.[1] First of all, the reasons why we went were that the Maquasen and Sinnekens had often come to our Commissary Marten Gerritsen[2] and me, saying that there were French Indians[3] in their country, and that they had called a truce with them, so that they, namely, the Maquasen, would trade furs with them there, because the Maquasen wanted as much for their furs as did the French Indians. Therefore, I asked Sr. Marten Gerritsen's permission to go there and learn the truth of the matter in order to report to their High Mightinesses[4] as soon as possible, because trade was going very badly. So for these reasons I went with Jeromus la Croex and Willem Tomassen. May the Lord bless our journey.

Between nine and ten o'clock we left with five Maquasen Indians mostly toward the northwest,[5] and at one half hour into the evening, after eight miles,[6] we came to a hunter's cabin[7] where we spent the night by the waterway that runs into their country, and is named Oÿoge.[8] The Indians here fed us venison. The country is mostly covered with pine trees and there is much flat land.[9] This waterway flows past their castle[10] in their coun-

1

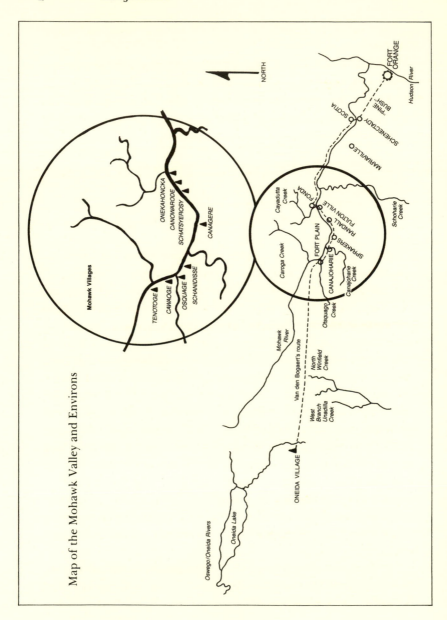

Map of the Mohawk Valley and Environs

try, but we were unable to travel on it because of the heavy flooding.

12 ditto. We continued our journey three hours before dawn. The Indians, who traveled with us, would have left us there, if I had not noticed it; and when we intended to eat something, their dogs had eaten up our meat and cheese so that we had nothing but dry bread to travel on. After we had traveled an hour, we came to the tributary[11] that flows into our river[12] and past the Maquase's villages. Here there was a heavy ice flow. Jeronimus crossed first in a canoe made of tree bark[13] with an Indian because only two men could travel together in it. After this Willem and I [crossed]. It was so dark that we could not see one another without staying close together so that it was not without danger. After crossing over, we went another one and a half miles and came to a hunter's cabin.[14] We entered and ate some venison there. We then continued our journey. After we had gone another half mile, we saw some people coming toward us. When they saw us, they ran away. Throwing down their bags and packs, they ran into a marsh and hid behind a thicket so that we were unable to see them. We looked at their goods and packs, taking a small loaf of bread baked with beans.[15] We ate it up and continued on mostly along this aforesaid waterway, which flowed most fiercely because of the flood. There are many islands in this waterway, on the banks of which are 500 or 600 morgens[16] of flatland; indeed, much more. When we, by estimation, had covered eleven miles, we came at one hour into the evening to a cabin one half mile from the first castle.[17] No one was there but women. We would have then continued on, but I could not move my feet because of the rough going; so, we slept there. It was very cold with a north wind.

13 ditto. In the morning we went together to the castle over the ice that had frozen in the waterway during the night. When we had gone one half mile, we came into their first castle that

stood on a high hill.[18] There were only 36 houses, row on row in the manner of streets, so that we easily could pass through. These houses are constructed and covered with the bark of trees, and are mostly flat above. Some are 100, 90, or 80 steps long; 22 or 23 feet high.[19] There were also some interior doors made of split planks furnished with iron hinges. In some houses we also saw ironwork: iron chains, bolts, harrow teeth, iron hoops, spikes, which they steal when they are away from here.[20] Most of the people were out hunting for bear and deer.[21] These houses were full of grain that they call ONESTI and we corn;[22] indeed, some held 300 or 400 skipples.[23] They make boats and barrels of tree-bark and sew with it.[24] We ate here many baked and boiled pumpkins which they called ANONSIRA.[25] None of the chiefs was at home, except for the most principal one called ADRIOCHTEN,[26] who was living one quarter mile from the fort in a small cabin because many Indians here in the castle had died of smallpox.[27] I invited him to come visit with me, which he did. He came and bid me welcome, and said that he wanted us to come with him very much. We would have gone but we were called by another chief when we were already on the path, and turned back toward the castle. He had a large fire started at once, and a fat haunch of venison cooked, from which we ate; and he also gave us two bear-skins to sleep on, and presented me with three beaver pelts.[28] In the evening I made some cuts with a knife on Willem Tomassen's leg, which had swollen from walking, and then smeared it with bear's grease. We slept here in this house, and ate large quantities of pumpkin, beans, and venison so that we suffered of no hunger here but fared as well as it is possible in their country. I hope that everything shall succeed.

14 ditto. Jeronimus wrote a letter to the commissary, Marten Gerritsen, asking for paper, salt, and ATSOCHWAT, i.e., Indian tobacco.[29] We went out with the chief to see if we could shoot some turkeys,[30] but got none. However, in the evening I bought

a very fat turkey for 2 hands of sewant,[31] which the chief cooked for us; and the grease that cooked from it he put in our beans and corn. This chief let me see his idol which was a marten's head with protruding teeth, covered with red duffel-cloth.[32] Others keep a snake, a turtle, a swan, a crane, a pigeon, and such similar objects for idols or telling fortunes; they think that they will then always have luck.[33] Two Indians left from here for Fort Orange with skins.

15 ditto. I went out again with the chief to hunt turkeys, but we got none. In the evening the chief once again let us see his idol. On account of the heavy snow over the path we decided to stay here another two or three days until the opportunity presented itself to proceed.

16 ditto. In the afternoon a good hunter named SICKARIS came here who wanted us to go with him very much and carry our goods to his castle. He offered to let us sleep in his house and stay there as long as we pleased. Because he offered us so much, I presented him with a knife and two awls; and to the chief in whose home we had stayed I presented a knife and a scissors.[34] Then we departed from this castle ONEKAHONCKA.[35] After we had gone one half mile over the ice we saw a village with only six houses. It was called CANOWARODE,[36] but we did not enter it because he said it was not worth much. After we had gone another half mile we passed a village with twelve houses called SCHATSYEROSY.[37] This one was like the other, saying also that it was not worth much. After we had gone a mile or a mile and a half past great tracts of flatland, we entered a castle at about two hours in the evening. I could see nothing else but graves.[38] This castle is called CANAGERE[39] and is situated on a hill without palisades or any defense.[40] There were only seven men at home and a group of old women and children.[41] The chiefs of this castle TONNOSATTON and TONIWEROT[42] were out hunting so that we slept in SECKARIS's house as he had promised us. We counted in his house 120 pelts of marketable

beaver that he had caught with his own hands.[43] We ate beaver's meat here everyday.[44] In this castle there are 16 houses, 50, 60, 70, 80 steps long, and one of 16 steps, and one of five steps in which a bear was being fattened. It had been in there almost three years and was so tame that it ate everything given it.[45]

17 ditto. Sunday. We looked over our goods and came upon a paper of sulphur. Jeronimus took some out and threw it on the fire. They saw the blue flame and smelled the odor, and told us that they also had such goods. When SICKARIS came in, they got it out and let us look at it, and it was the same. We asked him how he came by it. He told us that they got it from the foreign Indians, and that they considered it good for healing many illnesses, but principally for their legs when they became very sore from traveling and are very tired.[46]

18 ditto. Three women came here from the Sinnekens with some dried and fresh salmon, but they smelled very bad. They sold each salmon for one guilder[47] or two hands of sewant. They also brought much green tobacco to sell, and had been six days underway. They could not sell all their salmon here, but went with it to the first castle.[48] Then we were supposed to travel with them when they returned. In the evening Jeronimus told me that an Indian was planning to kill him with a knife.

December 19. We received a letter from Marten Gerritsen dated the eighteenth of this year.[49] With it came paper, salt, and tobacco for the Indians and a bottle of brandy. We hired a man to guide us to the Sinnekens, and gave him one half piece of duffel, two axes, two knives, and two awls. If it had been summer there would have been people enough to accompany us, but since it was winter they did not want to leave their country because it snowed there often a man's height deep. Today we had a very heavy rain. I gave this Indian a pair of shoes. His name was SQORHEA.[50]

December 20. Then we left the second castle, and when we had gone one mile our Indian SQORHEA came before a stream that we had to cross. This stream was running very hard with many large chunks of ice, because yesterday's heavy rain had broken up the stream so that we were in great danger. Had one of us just fallen, it would have been the end. But the Lord God protected us and we made it across. We were soaked up to the waist.[51] After going another half mile, with wet and frozen clothing, stockings, and shoes, we came to a very high hill on which stood 32 houses, all similar to the previous ones. Some were 100, 90, 80 steps or paces long. In each house there were four, five or six places for fires and cooking. There were many Indians at home here so that we caused much curiosity in the young and old; indeed, we could hardly pass through the Indians here. They pushed one another into the fire to see us. It was almost midnight before they left us. We could not do anything without having them shamelessly running about us. This is the third castle, and it is called SCHANIDISSE. The chief's name is TEWOWARY.[52] This evening I got a lion skin[53] to cover myself with; however, in the morning I had at least 100 lice. We ate here much venison. There is considerable flatland around and near this castle, and the woods are full of oak and walnut trees.[54] We got a beaver here in exchange for an awl.

December 21. We left very early in the morning, intending to go to the fourth castle. However, after we had gone a half mile we came to a village with nine houses called OSQUAGE.[55] The chief's name was OQUOHO, i.e., wolf.[56] Here there was a great stream which our guide would not cross.[57] Because of the heavy rain, the water was over our heads. For this reason we delayed until Saturday. This chief gave us many goods and fed us well, for everything in his house was at our disposal. He told me simply that I was his brother and good friend. Indeed, he also told me how he had traveled thirty days overland, and saw there an Englishman coming from the Minquas[58] in order to learn their language for the fur trade. I asked him whether there were French Indians near the Sinnekens. He said, yes,

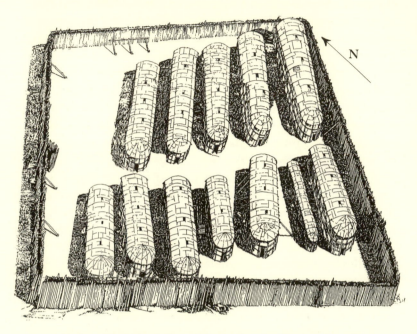

Fig. 6. Artist's depiction of the Mohawk village of Caughnawaga, c. 1666/7–1693, from the drawing by A. H. van Vliet, with permission of the Mohawk-Caughnawaga Museum, Fonda, N.Y.

and I was pleased, and thought that I would then reach my objective. I was asked here to heal a man who was very sick.[59]

December 22. In the morning at sunrise we crossed the stream together. It was over our knees and was so cold that our stockings and shoes quickly froze as hard as armor-plate. The Indians dared not cross there but went two by two with a stick from hand to hand. After we had gone one half mile, we came to a village called CAWAOGE.[60] It had 14 houses and a tame bear. We went in and smoked a pipe of tobacco because the

old man, who was our guide, was very tired. An old man came
to us and said, "Welcome, welcome, should you have to stay
overnight." However, we left in order to continue our journey.
I wanted to buy the bear, but they would not part with it. All
along the path stood many trees very similar to the savin tree.[61]
They have a very thick bark. This village is also located on a
high hill. After we had gone a mile overland through a sparsely
wooded region we came to the 4th castle called TENOTOGE.[62] It
had 55 houses, some 100 steps [in size] and others more or less
as large. The waterway that was mentioned earlier ran past
here and took the course mostly north-west and south-east.
There are more houses on the opposite bank of the waterway;[63]
however, we did not enter them because they were mostly full
of grain. The houses in this castle are full of grain and beans.[64]
Here the Indians looked on in amazement; for most everyone
was at home, and they crowded in on us so much that we could
barely pass among them.[65] After a long period, an Indian came
to us who took us to his house and we went in it. The castle
was surrounded with three rows of palisades. However, now
there were only 6 or 7 [posts] left, so thick that it was unbe-
lievable that Indians could do it.[66] They pushed one another
into the fire in order to see us.

23 Dec. A man came shouting and screaming through some
of the houses here. However, we did not know what it was
supposed to mean. After a while Jeronimus de la Croix came,
and wondered what it meant that the Indians were arming
themselves. I asked them what was meant by it and they said
[it was] nothing against me, "We are going to play with one
another." There were four with clubs, and some with axes and
sticks so that there were 20 men under arms; 9 on one side
and 11 on the other. Then they went at each other, fighting
and striking. Some wore armor and helmets which they made
themselves from thin reeds and cord woven together so that
no arrow or axe could penetrate to cause serious injury.[67] After

they had skirmished in this manner for a long time, the adversaries ran at one another; and the one dragged the other by the hair as they would do with conquered enemies, and would then cut their heads off.[68] They wanted us to fire our pistols, but we went away and left them.[69] Today we feasted on two bears, and we received today one half skipple of beans and some dried strawberries.[70] Also, we provided ourselves here with bread that we could take along on the journey. Some of it had nuts, chestnuts, dried blueberries and sunflower seeds baked in it.[71]

24 Dec. Since it was Sunday I looked in on a person who was sick. He had invited into his house two of their doctors who were supposed to heal him. They were called SUNACH-KOES.[72] As soon as they arrived, they began to sing, and kindled a large fire, sealing the house all around so that no draft could enter. Then both of them put a snakeskin around their heads and washed their hands and faces. They then took the sick person and laid him before the large fire. Taking a bucket of water in which they had put some medicine, they washed a stick in it ½ ell long.[73] They stuck it down their throats so that the end could not be seen, and vomited on the patient's head and all over his body. Then they performed many farces with shouting and rapid clapping of hands, as is their custom, with much display, first on one thing and then on the other, so that the sweat rolled off them everywhere.[74]

25 Dec. As it was Christmas day we arose early in the morning, intending to go to the Sinnekens. However, on account of the steady snow we were unable to start out, because no one would go with us to carry our goods. I asked them how many chiefs there were and they told me thirty persons.

26 Dec. This morning I was given two pieces of bear's meat to take on the journey. We took our leave amid much uproar that surged behind and before us. They repeatedly shouted: "ALLESE RONDADE," i.e., "Shoot!"[75] However, we did not want

to shoot. Finally they went away. Today we passed over much flatland, and also through a stream over our knees in depth. I think that we proceeded today mostly in a west-north-west direction. The woods through which we traveled were at first mostly oak but after three or four hours underway we encountered mostly birch.[76] It snowed the entire day so that it was very difficult to climb over the hills. After an estimated seven miles, we came to a bark hut in the woods where we kindled a fire and stayed the night. It continued to snow with a strong north wind. It was extremely cold.

Dec. 27. Early in the morning we continued on with great difficulty through two and a half feet of snow in some places. We went over hills, and through thickets, seeing tracks of many bear and elk,[77] but no Indians. Here there are beech trees.[78] After going seven or eight miles, we found at sunset once again a hut in the woods with little bark, but with some tree branches. We again made a big fire and cooked SAPPAEN.[79] It was so cold during the night that I could barely sleep two hours.

Dec. 28. We continued on, proceeding as before.[80] After we had gone one or two miles, we came to a waterway that the Indians told me flowed into the land of the Minquasen. After having gone another mile we came to another waterway that flowed into the South River, so the Indians told me.[81] Here many otters[82] and beavers were caught. Today we passed over many high hills. The woods are full of many large trees, but mostly birch. After going another seven or eight miles we did as above. It was extremely cold.

Dec. 29. We pushed on with our journey. After having traveled a while, we came to a very high hill. When we had just about reached the top, I fell so that I thought that I had broken my ribs; however, it was only the handle of my sword that had broken. We passed through low lands where many oak trees and ironwood grew.[83] After seven more miles, we found another hut into which we settled ourselves. We made a fire and ate up all the food we had, for the Indians said that we were still about four miles from the castle. It was nearly sunset when another Indian ran on to the castle to tell them that we were coming. We would have gone too, but because we were all very hungry the Indians would not take us along. Course NW.

Dec. 30. We proceeded toward the Sinnekens' castle without eating. After having gone a while, the Indians pointed out to me the tributary of the river before Fort Orange, which passes through the land of the Maquaesen.[84] A woman came along the way, bringing us baked pumpkins to eat. This stretch is mostly full of birch wood and flatlands cleared for sowing. Just before reaching the castle, we saw three graves in the manner of our graves: long and high. Otherwise their graves are round. These graves were surrounded with palisades that they had split from trees, and were so neatly made that it was a wonder. They were painted red, white, and black. Only the chief's grave had an entrance, above which stood a large wooden bird surrounded by paintings of dogs, deer, snakes, and other animals.[85] After having gone four or five miles, the Indians asked us to shoot. We fired our weapons, which we reloaded, and then we went to the castle. Northwest of us we saw a very large body of water. Opposite the water was extremely high ground which seemed to lie in the clouds.[86] When I inquired about it, the Indians told me that the French came into that water to trade.[87] After that we confidently went to the castle where the Indians divided themselves into two rows and let us pass in between them through their entrance.[88] The one we passed through was three and a half feet wide. Above the entrance stood three large wooden images, carved as men, by which three locks fluttered that they had cut from the heads of slain Indians as a token of truth, that is to say, victory. This castle has two entrances, one on the east and one on the west side. A lock was also hanging by the east gate, but this gate was one and half feet smaller than the other. Then we were finally brought into the farthest house, where I found many acquaintances. We were put in the place where the chief was accustomed to sit because he was not home at the time. We were cold, wet, and tired. We received food immediately, and they built a good fire. This castle is also located on a very high hill and was surrounded with two rows of palisades, 767 steps in circumference, in which there are 66 houses; but built much better and higher than all the others.[89] There were many wooden gables on the houses which were painted with all sorts of animals.[90] They sleep here mostly on raised platforms, more than any other Indians.[91] In the afternoon, one of the councillors[92] came to ask me what we were doing in his country and what we brought him for gifts. I said that we brought him nothing, but that we just came for a visit. However, he said that we were worth nothing because we brought him no gifts.[93] Then he told how the French had traded with them here with six men and had given them good gifts; for they had traded in the aforementioned river[94] last August of this year with six men. We saw there good timber axes, French shirts, coats, and razors. And this councillor derided us as scoundrels, and said that we were worthless because we gave them so little for their furs. They said that the French gave them six hands of sewant for one beaver and all sorts of other things in addition. The Indians sat so close to us here that we could barely sit. If they had wanted to do anything to us we could have done nothing, but there was no danger to our persons. In this river already mentioned, there are six or seven or even 800 salmon caught in one day. I saw houses with 60, 70 and more dried salmon.[95]

31 Dec. On Sunday the chief of this castle returned home. He was called ARENIAS. He came with another man, saying that they came from the French Indians. Some of the Indians gave a scream, saying JAWE ARENIAS,[96] which meant that they thanked him for coming. I told him that we would fire three shots this evening, and they said that it was good and they were very

pleased. We asked them for the locations of all of their castles and for their names, and how far they were from one another. They put down kernels of corn and stones, and Jeronimus made a map from them. We reckoned everything in miles; how far every place was from one another. The Indians here told us that in that high country that we had seen near the lake there lived people with horns.[97] They also said that many beavers were caught there; however, they dared not travel so far because of the French Indians. For this reason, therefore, they would make peace. This evening we fired three shots in honor of the year of our Lord and Redeemer JESU CHRISTO.[98]

PRAISE THE LORD ABOVE ALL
IN THE CASTLE ONNEYUTTEHAGE[99]
OR SINNEKENS   1635 January

1 January. An Indian once again called us scoundrels, as has been previously told, and he was very malicious so that Willem Tomassen became so angry that the tears ran from his eyes. The Indian seeing that we were upset, asked us why we looked at him with such anger. We were sitting during this time with their 46 persons around and near us. Had they had any malicious intentions, they could have easily grabbed us with their hands and killed us without much trouble. However, when I had heard his screaming long enough, I told him that he was the scoundrel. He began to laugh and said that he was not angry and said "You must not be angry. We are happy that you have come here." Jeronimus gave the chief two knives, two scissors, and some awls and needles that we had with us. In the evening the Indians hung up a belt of sewant and some other strung sewant that the chief had brought back from the French Indians as a token of peace that the French Indians were free to come among them; and they sang HO SCHENE JO HO HO SCHENE

I ATSIEHOENE ATSIHOENE.[100] Whereupon all the Indians shouted three times NETHO NETHO NETHO,[101] and then hung up another belt, singing KATON KATON KATON KATON.[102] Then they shouted in a loud voice HŸ HŸ HŸ.[103] After long deliberation they concluded the peace for four years, and then each went to his house.

Jan. 2. The Indians came to us and said that we had to wait another four or five days; and if we could not go sooner, then they would provide us with all necessities. However, I said that we could not wait long. They answered that they had sent for the ONNEDAEGES,[104] which is the castle[105] next to them. But I said that they mostly let us starve, whereupon they said that henceforth we would receive sufficient food. Today we were twice invited to feast on bear's meat and salmon.

January 3. Some old men came to us and said that they wanted to be our friends, and that we must not be afraid. Whereupon I told them that we were not afraid. Toward midday they gathered their council here with 24 men. After they had conferred for a long time, an old man came to me and felt whether my heart was beating against his hand. When he shouted that we were not afraid, six more men came from the council, and they presented us with a beaver coat. They gave it to me saying, "It is for your journey, because you are so tired." And pointing to my feet and his, said, "That is also because you have walked through the snow." When we accepted it, they shouted three times NETHO NETHO NETHO, which means that they were pleased. At once they laid five more beaver skins at my feet, and thereby requested that they would like to have four hands of sewant and four hands of long cloth[106] for each large beaver because "We have to travel so far with our pelts and when we arrive we often find no cloth, no sewant, no axes, kettles or anything else; and thus we have labored in vain. Then we have to go back a long way carrying our goods." After we had sat for a time, an old man came to us for whom they translated us

Fig. 7. *t'Fort Nieuw Amsterdam op de Manhatans* [The Hart-
gens View of Manhattan], 1626–1628, from *Beschrijvinghe
Van Virginia Nieuw Nederlandt*, Amsterdam.

in another language,[107] and he said, "You have not said whether
we shall have four hands or not." Whereupon I told him that
we had no authority to promise them that, but that we would
tell the chief at the Manhatas,[108] who was our commander,[109]
and that I would inform him of everything in the spring, and
come myself into their country. Then they said to me WELS-
MACHKOO,[110] "You must not lie, and come in the spring to us
and bring us all an answer. If we receive four hands, then we
shall trade our pelts with no one else." Then they gave me the
five beavers and shouted again in a loud voice NETHO NETHO
NETHO; and so that everything should be firm and binding, they
shouted or sang: HA ASSIRONI ATSIMACHKOO KENT OYAKAYING
WEE ONNEYATTE ONAONDAGE KOYOCKWE HOO SENOTO WANY-

AGWEGANNE HOO SCHENEHALATON KASTEN KANOSONI YNDICKO,[111] which was to say that I should go to all these places, by naming all the castles, and I would go there freely and be free there in every place; I would have house and fire, wood and anything else. Whatever I received there would be mine; and if I wished to go to the French, then they would go with me and bring me back wherever I desired. Thereupon they again shouted in a loud voice three times, NETHO NETHO NETHO, and I was again made a present of a beaver. This day we were invited to eat bear's meat. In this chief's house three or four meals were eaten everyday. Whatever was not cooked there was brought in from other houses in large kettles, because the council came here everyday to eat; and whosoever is in the house, receives a wooden bowl full of food, for it is the custom that every man who comes here, receives a bowl full. If bowls are lacking, then they bring their own bowls and spoons. They then sit down next to one another where the bowls are fetched and brought back full, because an invited guest does not stand up until he has eaten. Sometimes they sing and sometimes not. They then thank the host and each returns home[112]

Jan. 4. Two men came to me and said that I should come and see how they would drive out the devil; but I said that I had seen that before. However, I had to go along anyway. There were twelve men here who were to drive him out; and because I would not go alone, I took Jeronimus with me. When we arrived, the floor of the house was completely covered with tree bark over which the devil-hunters were to walk. They were mostly old men who were all colored or painted with red paint on their faces because they were to perform something strange. Three of them had garlands around their heads upon which were five white crosses. These garlands were made of deer's hair which they dyed with the roots of herbs. In the middle of this house was a very sick person who had been languishing for a long time, and there sat an old woman who had an empty turtle shell in her hands, in which were beads that rattled while she sang.[113] Here they intended to catch the devil and trample him to death, for they stomped all the bark in the house to pieces, so that none remained whole. Wherever they saw but a little dust on the corn, they beat at it with great excitement, and then they blew that dust toward one another and were so afraid that each did his best to flee as if he had seen the devil.[114] After much stomping and running, one of them went to the sick person and took an otter from his hand, and for a long time sucked on the sick man's neck and back. Then he spit in the otter and threw it on the ground, running away with great excitement. Other men then ran to the otter and performed such antics that it was a wonder to see; indeed, they threw fire, ate fire, and threw around hot ashes and embers in such a way that I ran out of the house.[115] Today I received another beaver.

Jan 5 I bought four dried salmon and two pieces of bear's meat that was nine inches thick; there was some here even thicker. Today we ate beans cooked with bear's meat. Otherwise nothing occurred.

Jan. 6. Nothing in particular happened other than I was shown some stones with which they make fire when they go into the woods, and which are scarce. These stones would also be good on firelocks.[116]

Jan. 7 We received a letter[117] from Marten Gerritsz dated the last of December by a Sinck[118] who came from our fort. He said that our people were very troubled because we did not return, thinking that we had been killed. We ate here fresh salmon that had been caught but two days ago. Six and a half fathoms of sewant were stolen from our bags and never recovered.

Jan. 8 ARENIAS came to me and said that he would accompany me to our fort with all his pelts for trading. Jeronimus offered to sell his coat here but could not get rid of it.

Jan. 9 The ONNEDAGENS[119] arrived here in the evening; six

old men and four women, who were very tired from the journey. They brought some beaver pelts with them. I went and thanked them for coming to visit us. They welcomed me and because it was late I went again to our house.

Jan. 10 Jeronimus badly burned his pants that had fallen from his body into the fire during the night. The chief's mother gave him cloth to repair them and Willem Tomassen sewed them up again.

Jan. 11 The Indians came to me at 10 o'clock in the morning and said, "Come into the house where the ONNEDAGENS sit in council and shall give you gifts." Jeronimus and I went there and took along a pistol. We sat down by an old man named CANASTOGEERA,[120] who was about 55 years old. He said to us, "Friends, I have come here to see you and to speak with you." We thanked him for this, and after they held council for a long time, an interpreter came to me and gave me five wild beavers for my journey and because we came to visit them. I took the beavers and thanked them, whereupon they shouted loudly three times NETHO, and then they laid another five wild beavers at my feet and gave them to us because we had come into his council house. We would have received many pelts as gifts, if we had just come into his country, and he asked me earnestly to visit his country in the summer. Then they gave me another four wild beavers and demanded that they must receive more for their pelts, then they would bring us many pelts. If I returned to their country in the summer, we would have three or four Indians to show us that lake and where the French came to trade with their sloops.[121] When we picked up our fourteen beavers they shouted once again three times NETHO, and we fired three shots and gave the chiefs two pair of knives, some awls, and needles. Then we received the news that we could go. We still had five pieces of salmon and two pieces of bear's meat to eat on the way, and we were given here some bread and meal to take along.

Jan. 12 We said goodbye, and when we thought that everything was ready, the Indians would not carry our goods: 28 beavers and five salmon with some bread, because they all had enough to carry. However, after much grumbling and nice words, they went with us in company, carrying our goods. There were many people here who walked along with us shouting ALLE SARONDADE, that is to say, "Shoot!"[122] When we passed the chief's grave, we fired three shots, and then they left us and went away. It was about nine o'clock when we left here. We walked only about five miles through two and a half feet of snow. It was very difficult going so that some Indians had to sleep in the woods in the snow, but we found a hut where we slept.

Jan. 13 Early next morning we were once again on our way. After going another seven or eight miles, we came to a hut where we stopped to cook something to eat, and to sleep. ARENIAS pointed out to me a place on a high hill and said after a ten days' journey we could come to a river there where many people lived and where there were many cows and horses. However, we must sail across the river for a whole day and then travel another six days to get there.[123] This was the place we passed on the 29th of December. He did us much good.

Jan. 14 On Sunday we were ready to go, but the chief wanted to stay in order to go out bear hunting from here. However, because it was nice weather, I went on alone with two or three Indians. Two Maquaesen came to us here because they wanted to go to trade elk skins and SATTEEU.[124]

Jan. 15 In the morning two hours before daybreak, after having eaten with the Indians, I continued my journey. When it was almost dark, the Indians built a fire in the woods for they would go no farther. About three hours into evening I came to a hut where I had slept on December 26th. It was very cold and I was not able to start a fire. Therefore I had to walk around the whole night to keep warm.

Jan. 16 In the morning three hours before daybreak, when the moon came up, I looked for the path, which I finally found. At nine in the morning after hard going, I came to a great flat country. After transversing a high hill I came upon a very level path which was made by the Indians who had passed here with much venison when returning home from the hunt to their castles. I saw the castle at ten o'clock and entered it at twelve noon. At least 100 people accompanied me in and showed me a house where I was to stay. They gave me a white hare[125] to eat which they had caught two days ago. It was cooked with chestnuts. I received a piece of wheat bread from an Indian who had come from Fort Orange on the 15th of this month. Toward evening about 40 fathoms of sewant were distributed among them as testimony of the Indians who had died of the smallpox; this in the presence of the chiefs and nearest friends, because it is their custom that they distribute it thus to the chiefs and nearest friends.[126] Toward evening the Indians gave me two bear skins with which to cover myself, and they fetched reeds to put under me. I was also told that our people longed for our return.

Jan. 17 Jeronimus and Willem Tomassen arrived at the castle TENOTOGEHAGE[127] with some other Indians. They were still alert and healthy. In the evening another 100 fathoms of sewant were distributed to the chiefs and friends of closest blood.

Jan. 18 We went again to this castle, that is to say, from this castle to hasten our progress homeward. Although there were in some houses here at least 40 or 50 quarters of venison, cut and dried, they offered us little of it to eat. After proceeding a half mile, we passed through the village called KAWAOGE;[128] and a half mile further we came to the village of OSQUAGO.[129] The chief OSQUAHOO[130] received us well. We waited here for the chief AROMYAS[131] whom we had left in the castle of TENO-TOOGE.

Jan. 19 In the morning we continued our journey with all haste. After traveling a half mile we came to the third castle called SCHANADISSE.[132] I looked into some houses to see whether there were any pelts. I found nine ONNEDAGES there with pelts whom I asked to accompany me to the second castle. The chief TATUROT[133] was at home, that is to say, TONEWEROT was at home, who pronounced us welcome at once and gave us a very fat quarter of venison which we cooked. As we were sitting eating we received a letter from Marten Gerrtsen[134] by an Indian who was looking for us. It was dated the 8th of this month. We decided unanimously to proceed to the first castle as quickly as possible in order to depart for Fort Orange in the morning. We arrived at the first castle while the sun was still three hours high. We had bread baked here and packed the three other beavers that we had received from the chief when we first came here. We ate and slept here this night.

Jan. 20 In the morning before daybreak, Jeronimus sold his coat to an old man for four beavers. We left this place one hour before dawn. When we had covered about two miles, the Indians pointed to a high hill where their castle had stood nine years ago when they were driven out by the Mahicans.[135] Since that time they had not wanted to live there any longer. After traveling seven or eight miles, we found that the hunter's cabin had been burned so that we had to spend the night under the stars.

Jan. 21 Early in the morning we started out once again. After traveling for some time, we came upon a wrong path that was the most traveled, but because the Indians knew the paths better than we, they went back with us. After going eleven miles we came, praise and thank God, to Fort Orange the 21st of January Anno 1635.

Notes

1. The term *Maquasen,* commonly *Maquas,* is a reference to the Mohawk, the easternmost tribe of the Five Nations Iroquois. Many forms appear in the literature, e.g., DeLaet [1625] records *Mackwaes* (Jameson 1909, p. 47), Megapolensis [1644] *Mahakimbas* (Jameson 1909, p. 172), Michaelius [1628] *Maechibaeys* (Jameson 1909, p. 31), Van Laer (1924, p. 80), *Macquaes,* and others. "The most etymologically correct early spelling is Mohowawogs, 1638 (Roger Williams), which has the English plural -s added to a Narrangansett or Massachusett word for 'man-eaters', cognate with Unami *mhuwé·yɔk* 'cannibal monsters' " (Fenton and Tooker 1978, p. 478). To distinguish themselves from the other Iroquois, the Mohawk referred to themselves as *kaynv-ʔkehró:nu* or *kanvyʔkehá:ka,* 'the flint people' or 'people of the place of the flint'. Compare Ives Goddard's synonymy in Fenton and Tooker (1978) for additional detail.

The word *Sinnekens* functioned for the Dutch and others as a generic applied to all of those Indians west of the Mohawk (Hewitt 1910), that is, the "upper Iroquois," although in this context the journalist is referring to the Oneida, the Iroquoian group adjacent to the Mohawk tribe.

Note: Unless otherwise indicated, all transcriptions left in the original Iroquoian language cited throughout these endnotes are Mohawk, with the exception perhaps of a few words which Van den Bogaert may have picked up at Oneida where he was from December 30 to January 12. For example, the word SCHENEHALATON (see note 111) has Oneida "l" instead of Mohawk "r."

2. The commissary was responsible for the stores at West India

23

Company trading posts, such as Fort Orange, as well as being commander of the fort.

3. The "French Indians" were Indians allied to or in a trading relationship with the French. They included Algonquian and Iroquoian-speaking bands and tribes situated in northern New England and eastern Canada.

4. This is a reference to authorities in the Netherlands, here either the directors of the West India Company or the States General (refer to Introduction).

5. The route taken by Van den Bogaert and his companions into the Mohawk Valley has been described often (cf. Frey 1898; Beauchamp 1900; Reid 1901; Ruttenber 1906; Greene 1925; Lathers and Sheehan 1937; Clarke 1940; Carse 1949; Grassmann 1969). In all of these cases there are problems in the interpretation of the journal which lead to inaccuracies regarding the route taken. Refer to the map (p. 2) as references are made in the notes to the party's progress. See note 18 for a detailed discussion of the first part of their journey.

Upon leaving Fort Orange with five Mohawk guides, Van den Bogaert notes that their direction was toward the northwest. This would have sent them across vast flatlands consisting of flood and sand plains and dominated by white pine, pitch pine, and oak forests, the so-called "Pine Bush" (Dineen 1975; Reilly 1975, p. 9), placing them near the present city of Schenectady, New York.

6. Van den Bogaert estimates and records distances traveled while on his journey. His unit of measurement is *mylen* (miles). The definitive Dutch dictionary *Woordenboek der Nederlandsche Taal* notes that a *mijl* is 5,600 ells (Kluyver 1904, v. 9, p. 705). An "old Dutch" ell is 27 inches; therefore, a Dutch *mijl* is 2.4 statute miles. Others contend that a Dutch *mijl* is equivalent to about three English miles, a seventeenth-century English mile being approximately 5,000 feet. Accordingly, a Dutch *mijl* would be 15,000 feet or 2.8 statute miles (cf. Sewell 1754; Van der Donck 1968, pp. 10, 141). However, Jameson (1909, p. 138) maintains that Van den Bogaert was using a Dutch league, "nearer two English miles than three, as would be natural to one making his way for the first time through the wilderness." Calisch's (1875, p. 430) definition is derived from a different manner of reckoning, stating that a *mijl* equals one and one-quarter hour's walk, probably something over 2 statute miles.

Although Greene (1925, p. 221) contends that Van den Bogaert was an "explorer who evidently knew the forest, its trails and distances," the question of distances is moot. Given current archaeological information regarding the locations of Mohawk villages encountered by the Dutchmen and details of the geography of the valley, Van den Bogaert's estimates are clearly inaccurate and of no real value in pinpointing his position or the sites of Indian settlements as he proceeded on his journey. Moreover, recognizing that Van den Bogaert was a barber-surgeon and not an explorer, and consequently aware of little outside the environs of Fort Orange, does not enhance his ability to judge distances. It must be remembered that he was traveling during the winter, fighting through deep snow as he was led up hill and down dale. As a Dutchman he would have been at a disadvantage in guessing distances in hilly and mountainous terrain. This, added to his tortuous path, would make any estimates difficult, to say the least.

7. The "hunter's cabin" encountered by Van den Bogaert, and other isolated cabins mentioned later in this and subsequent journal entries, are in all likelihood trail houses. Parker (1923, p. 283, general note) discusses "'trail houses,' which were erected at intervals along the trails throughout Iroquois country, and in which food and other necessities were left by travelers who had used the shelter. Inquiry brought out the fact that these public hospices were common in the old days and were frequently built in response to dreams."

8. *Oÿoge. Ohiò:ke* 'On the river' is not found in modern Mohawk. Informants in Kahnawake thought it was possibly a Seneca word. In 1646, this term was used in reference to the Hudson River (JR, v. 29, p. 49).

The directional preposition "into" used by Van den Bogaert is incorrect. From his vantage point, the Mohawk River would flow "out of" the Mohawk's country. A similar difficulty is discussed in note 81.

9. This description of the country fits well with the "Pine Bush" region between present-day Albany and Schenectady (see note 5). In fact, the name Schenectady is derived from a Mohawk word *skahnéhtati* meaning literally 'it is beyond the pines'. Beauchamp (1907, p. 199) states "Schen-ec-ta-dy was properly the name of Albany, but was soon placed here [Schenectady], being equally significant in coming from the east."

10. The term "castle" denotes a large village (see note 17).

11. The Mohawk River. From Van den Bogaert's description, it is apparent that on December 11, the party approached the Mohawk River, found it heavily flooded, and unable to or not choosing to cross, spent the night. Early the next day they moved west, generally along

the river, but not in view of it, and again made an approach, this time at a place where they could cross safely.

12. The Hudson River.

13. The typical Iroquois canoe was not the sleek birch bark vessel used by the more northern Algonquian groups or the Huron. Instead, their canoes were constructed of the bark of the white and red elm (*Ulmus americana* and *Ulmus rubra*). Apparently, the relative scarcity and lack of sufficient size of the paper birch (*Betula papyrifera*) and the abundance of elm dictated the use of the latter material. Elm bark canoes were rather clumsy and unwieldy craft carrying up to six individuals, although larger craft are known. For early descriptions of Iroquois canoes and their method of manufacture, see Lafitau (1977, pp. 124–26) and Benson (1966, v. 1, p. 363). For additional information refer to Morgan (1962, pp. 367–69), Fenton and Dodge (1949), and Adney and Chappelle (1964, pp. 213–19).

14. The Dutchman probably crossed the Mohawk River somewhere in the vicinity of the cluster of islands near the present cities of Schenectady and Scotia (see map). This route is clearly the most direct between Fort Orange and the Mohawk Valley. Also, the Mohawk River swings north here, and it is reasonable to assume that the party would have avoided going any farther north than necessary (see note 16).

In 1642, Arent van Curler traveled into the valley in hopes of securing the release of the Jesuit father Isaac Jogues and his companions who were being held captive by the Mohawk. On his return, Van Curler commented on "the most beautiful land" situated on the Mohawk River "half a days journey from the colonie [Fort Orange]" (O'Callaghan 1846, v. 1, p. 464). In 1661, he and several others purchased this tract from the Mohawk and founded the settlement of Schenectady (Trelease 1960, p. 136). It is very likely that Van Curler followed the same trail that Van den Bogaert had, one that led in a northwest direction from Fort Orange. Morgan (1962, p. 47) mentions an Indian trail that connected the site of Albany to the Mohawk River near Schenectady (cf. Huey 1975, p. 7).

15. This description matches the general appearance of corn bread prepared today by modern Iroquois. This staple and other prepared foods mentioned throughout the journal conform also to those in Parker (1910) and Waugh (1916).

Beans (*Phaseolus*) (see note 70).

16. Van den Bogaert's observation that there were many islands

in this stretch of the river securely establishes that the party had initially crossed the Mohawk in the vicinity of Schenectady and Scotia (see note 14). Prior to canalization, there were nearly a score of islands in the river from this point to about the mouth of the Schoharie Creek. From the Schoharie west, no islands would have been encountered until about six miles upriver from Fonda, above the "Noses," and beyond where the Dutchmen recrossed the river to the south side (see map) (Wright 1811; Hutchinson 1834; O'Callaghan 1850, v. 3, pp. 659–70).

Morgen is a Dutch land measurement. A Rhineland *morgen* is equivalent to 2.1 acres, while an Amsterdam *morgen* is slightly less, 2.06 acres (Van Laer 1908, p. 847).

17. Castle (Dutch, *casteel*). The Dutch distinguished between two settlement types: the castle and the village. Castles were apparently larger settlements, often fortified with a surrounding palisade, and located on hills above the river. The application of the term "castle" corresponds to the European usage and definition, i.e., a fortified place. The term "village" appears to have been used to identify smaller unfortified settlements or hamlets (cf. Abler 1970, p. 25). For the Mohawk, these were located at lower elevations and nearer the river. In times of danger the populations in these hamlets might have moved to the fortified and more secure castles (cf. Abler 1970, pp. 25–28) (see note 66).

18. The geographical locations of the Mohawk settlements visited by Van den Bogaert have been sought since the journal's initial publication. The literature cited in note 5 offers a variety of conclusions. In all cases, each author attempted to mark off the distances estimated between settlements as recorded in the journal, correlating these with the physiographic details provided for each locale; for example, situated on a "high hill," or near a "big stream." This information was then compared to what was known or believed to be true regarding historical and archaeological data and their interpretation. The results, reflecting the varying expertise of these individuals, are less than satisfactory and at times in error and should be used with caution.

For example, Reid (1901), working from questionable sources and with little critical insight, incorrectly places the first settlement, *Onekahoncka* (see note 35), near present-day Mariaville, and the second castle, *Canagere* (see note 39), east of Schoharie Creek, far from their probable locations. A less than careful reading of the journal by Greene

(1925), and his reliance on the work of a local antiquarian named Mr. Fea, caused him to place one village at the site of the former Montgomery County Home, north of the river and west of Fonda. All other settlements described by him are situated on the south side of the river. Clarke (1940), using Greene as a source for his own work, also places one village on the north side of the Mohawk in spite of the fact that Van den Bogaert is consistent in his observation that the villages were all on one side. Finally, Carse (1949, p. 7) writes that "at the time of Van Corlear's [Van den Bogaert's] journey in 1634, probably all of the Mohawk 'castles' were east of the modern city of Canajoharie." How such a conclusion was drawn is difficult to imagine given the well-known locations of the large streams Van den Bogaert crossed as he moved into the valley.

Other than showing where previous writers may have erred in identifying village sites, our new translation still does not provide for the precise identification of these settlements visited by Van den Bogaert. Neither does our current archaeological understanding of the area. Guesses by any number of amateur archaeologists regarding the identification of the settlements are the result of unsystematic and nonscientific work and are presently inadequate. Compounding the problem, their data remain unpublished and are, for the most part, inaccessible. A long-term archaeological research project begun by Snow and Starna (1980) in 1982, and continued by Snow since 1984, will eventually solve this vexing problem.

In the journal, the group recrossed the river to the south side over ice (ice floes?) which had frozen during the night. It is likely that the river at this point was relatively deep and slow moving, allowing the floes to freeze solidly enough to allow for safe passage. A document dated 1792 (O'Callaghan 1850, v. 3, pp. 659–70) details a survey of the Mohawk River made prior to canalization. In it is described a rift at Caughnawaga, west of Fonda. From the mouth of the Schoharie Creek to this rift, a distance of approximately six miles, the river was described as "very good water, deep and gently [sic]." Both above and below this section were rapids and rifts, a less than favorable condition for water or ice floes to freeze rapidly, i.e., overnight. Ruttenber (1906, p. 196) observed that the rapids and rifts just east of the mouth of Schoharie Creek were never known to have frozen in such a short period of time. Therefore, it is possible that it was somewhere in this section of the river where the group crossed to what was the first castle.

There is no evidence that the Schoharie Creek was encountered directly by the Dutchmen.

Van den Bogaert states that on December 12 they left a hunter's cabin in the Pine Bush three hours before dawn (c. 4:15 A.M. In this region the winter sun would have risen at 7:17 A.M. on December 12), traveled one hour (5:15 A.M.), and crossed the Mohawk River to the north shore (an estimated one-half hour to accomplish this, making their departure from the river c. 5:45 A.M.). They traveled a distance, stopping at another hunter's cabin where they ate (spending an estimated one-half hour) and then resumed their journey. At one hour into the evening (c. 5:15 P.M.—for the Dutch evening began at sunset, which occurred at 4:22 P.M. on December 12)—they stopped at a cabin one-half mile from the first castle. The amount of time spent traveling is between eleven and twelve hours. Assuming a walking speed of about two miles per hour, a reasonable rate considering the conditions, they would have traveled about twenty-two to twenty-four miles generally west from the place where they had first crossed the Mohawk River. They do not appear to have passed beyond Fonda, and most likely crossed to the south shore at a point at or just east of this village. This is concluded from negative evidence; that is, there is no mention of the party having encountered Cayadutta Creek, a large tributary running south into the Mohawk River on the western edge of Fonda. In the journal Van den Bogaert is careful to note the presence of large streams. Based on his consistency in this regard, if he had crossed the Cayadutta, it is improbable that he would have failed to mention it.

With the knowledge that the river was crossed initially between Scotia and Schenectady, that the distance traveled along the north side was considerable, and that they recrossed the river over the ice to the first castle, in addition to current archaeological information, it is possible to hypothesize the approximate position of the first settlement, *Onekahoncka*, placing it near Fultonville. Evidence exists for several village sites just west of here in the vicinity of Stone Ridge. It may be that one of these is the site of *Onekahoncka*. Only further archaeological investigations, however, can verify this.

19. The houses described by Van den Bogaert are typical of the "longhouses" of Northern Iroquoian populations. In general, such houses were approximately 20 to 25 feet wide, with lengths varying from 40 to more than 200 feet, the average being about 90 to 100 feet long (Van den Bogaert estimated the lengths of the houses by

simply stepping them off). Poles made from saplings, several inches in diameter, were set in the ground following a generally rectangular floor plan (figure 6). The tops of these poles were drawn together and secured, forming vertical or near-vertical walls and an arched or arborlike roof 15 to 20 feet high. Once this framework was erected, it was covered with sheets of elm bark, leaving an entrance, usually one at each end. Movable bark sheets at the apex of the roof could be adjusted to provide for light and ventilation. The interiors of the houses were divided into compartments placed along each side with a central aisle the length of the house. Hearths, placed in the aisle, were shared by occupants in opposing compartments. The compartments constituted a module of about 20–25 feet in length within the house. Each of these compartments housed a nuclear family, while the whole house was the residential unit for a household or matrilineage. Matrilineages are consanguineal kin groups composed of people who trace their descent through related females. This unit of social organization is fundamental to Iroquois society (Morgan 1962; Fenton 1978). There was often a storage area at either one or both ends of the longhouse. In addition, storage space was available between compartments and in and among sleeping platforms built against the house wall within each compartment. These platforms, generally constructed one or more feet off the ground to avoid dampness, cold, and vermin, were sometimes covered with reed mats or animal skins. At the same time, bark sheets and mats used for sleeping or sitting were placed on the house floor below these platforms. Descriptions of Iroquoian longhouses are found in Lafitau (1977, pp. 19–23), Bartram (1973, pp. 58–59), and Morgan (1962, 1881), with detailed summaries appearing in Tooker (1964), Heidenreich (1971), Trigger (1969, 1976), Fenton (1978), and Starna (1980).

20. The presence of iron materials among the Mohawk is interesting but not surprising. As early as 1580, European trade goods were being obtained by Mohawk raiding parties in the St. Lawrence Valley (Trigger 1978), although they first appear in small numbers on Mohawk sites about 1550 (Lenig 1977, p. 73). More direct availability followed the establishment of a Dutch settlement at Fort Nassau near present-day Albany in 1614. By 1624, Fort Orange provided nearly all trade goods to the Mohawk.

The iron materials Van den Bogaert saw do not, for the most part, represent the normal fare of trade items. Nails (spikes), hinges, and bolts, however, were being manufactured in Rensselaerswyck at about this time and may have found their way to the Mohawk (Van Laer 1908, p. 351; cf. Bradley 1979).

The interior doors of split planks and iron hinges reflect European influence on house construction. Interior transverse partitions with doorways usually covered with bark sheets or animal skins were common. They formed cubicles at one or both ends of the longhouse, areas used for storage of food and firewood, and also providing a space that would have helped reduce heat loss (Heidenreich 1971, pp. 118–20).

21. Although hunting among Northern Iroquoian Indians was a year-round endeavor, there was a seasonal emphasis on deer. A number of sources indicate that white-tailed deer (*Odocoileus virginianus*)—the major source of meat (venison) and hides—were hunted in late fall and early winter (cf. Tooker 1964, p. 65; Heidenreich 1971, p. 205; Gramly 1977; Fenton 1978, pp. 300–301; Kirkland 1980, p. 180). There also appears to have been a late winter deer hunt, probably during the month of March (Heidenreich 1971, p. 205; Trigger 1976, p. 39; Kirkland 1980, p. 104).

Bear (Black bear, *Ursus americanus*) (see note 45).

22. *Onesti.* Corn is *ó:nvhste?* in modern Mohawk and is the most important and popular of the domesticated plants used by the Iroquois (Waugh 1916; Parker 1910; Heidenreich 1971). Although there are no comparable figures for the Iroquois, Heidenreich (1971, p. 163) estimates that for each Huron person, approximately 65 percent of the daily caloric intake and 43 percent of the daily bulk intake was from corn. However, there was probably somewhat less an emphasis placed on this grain in the Iroquois diet due to the fact that hunting was more important and played a larger dietary role than for the Huron (Fenton 1978, p. 298).

23. Skipples (Dutch, *schepel*). A Dutch dry measure equivalent to .764 bushels (Van Laer 1908, p. 849).

24. Much of the material culture of the Iroquois was constructed of tree bark and other woody material (Beauchamp 1905; Lafitau 1974, 1977; Morgan 1962; Speck 1945; Fenton 1978).

25. *Anonsira.* The modern Mohawk equivalent is *onu?úsera?* 'squash'.

26. *Adriochten.* This individual is identified as "the most principal" chief in the village. He may have been a sachem, a League chief of the Mohawk, although there were other kinds of chiefs present in each village. Sachems (*rotiyá:ner*) were male individuals who were cho-

sen and appointed by the ranking women in a maternal household (matrilineage) or family (Fenton 1978, p. 314; Trigger 1969, p. 9). Their authority extended to civil matters in the village, to the tribe, and to the League, the governmental structure encompassing all five of the Iroquois tribes (Mohawk, Oneida, Onondaga, Cayuga, and Seneca). For detailed discussions of Iroquois political organization see Lafitau (1974, 1977), Morgan (1962), Fenton (1950, 1978), and Tooker (1978).

This chief's name is *ateryóhtu* in modern Mohawk. It contains the verb *-ryoht-* 'to die from something', found for instance in *yakoryóhtha?* 'one dies from it' or 'poison'. One native speaker suggested that a close literal translation of this name might be 'he has caused others to die'. This interpretation, taken in the context that this chief lived one-quarter of a mile from his village because many of the Indians there had died from smallpox, implies that *Adriochten* was perhaps in some way blamed for the epidemic and had been subsequently exiled. In this case, *Adriochten* could have been a nickname of sorts. Incidentally, *Adriochten* may be identical with *Saggodryochta*, head chief of the Mohawk, who in the summer of 1633 had traded pelts at Fort Orange (Grassmann 1969, p. 45).

27. Like other North American Indian populations, the Mohawk suffered greatly from a series of epidemics that resulted from contact with Europeans. Introduced diseases such as smallpox, measles, typhus, and others were particularly devastating. Indian populations had no immunity to these Old World pathogens and went into rapid decline. It is likely that the Mohawk experienced their initial epidemic in the second or third decade of the seventeenth century, although this may have occurred earlier (Dobyns 1983; cf. Snow and Starna 1984). It was at this time that they found themselves in frequent and often prolonged contact with the Dutch citizens near Fort Orange. In addition, exposure to Algonquian groups in the Hudson Valley and parts of New England, who had suffered earlier epidemics, would have been a contributing factor (Brasser 1978a; Heidenreich 1971; Starna 1980; Snow 1980; Snow and Starna 1984; Trigger 1985).

28. Beaver pelts were an important exchange commodity for Indians and Europeans (cf. Hunt 1940; Trelease 1960) (see note 44).

29. The letter written by Jeronimus dela Croix does not survive, nor does the map he drew (see entry of December 13). A manuscript and accompanying map, purported to be that of Dela Croix, found in a parcel of documents bequeathed to L. G. van Loon and subse-

quently translated and published by him (Van Loon 1939–1940), have been determined to be fakes (Gehring and Starna 1984).

According to Van den Bogaert, Dela Croix asked for not only salt and paper, but also tobacco (*Nicotiana rustica*), *atsochwat*.

Atsochwat does not mean Indian tobacco. It contains the verb root -*atshokw*- 'to have a smoke'. 'I smoke' is *katshókwas*. The modern Mohawk equivalent for tobacco is *oyừ:kwaʔ*.

The request for salt, probably wanted as a condiment, suggests that it was not used for this purpose among the Mohawk. In fact, such practice is not reported for the Northern Iroquoians (Fenton 1978, p. 298). The *Jesuit Relations* support this contention (JR, v. 6, p. 267; v. 7, p. 45; 18, p. 17) as does Sagard (1968, pp. 80, 112). There appear conflicting statements regarding the use of salt as a preservative. It is mentioned as a preservative for moose tongues in the *Relations* of 1647 (JR, v. 31, p. 281), although in 1653, Bressani (JR, v. 38, p. 245) comments that the Indians lacked salt to preserve game or fish.

30. Wild turkeys (*Meleagris gallopavo*) once abounded in the Northeast and were a popular food item (Grayson 1974; Ritchie 1969).

31. *Sewant* is from *sewan*, in a Long Island Algonquian dialect (Fenton 1971, p. 441). This term is synonymous with "wampum," cylindrical shell beads with a central aperture, strung into strings or woven into belts. Early on, the beads were made from several species of marine shell, especially the whelk (*Buccinum undatum*), the source for white beads, and the hard-shelled clam (*Venus mercenaria* L.), the source for purple beads. True wampum, that is, cylindrical and not discoidal beads, first appears in Iroquoia in the sixteenth century, having been obtained through trade. At this time it functioned in a ceremonial or ritual context. It does not seem to have at first been used as Indian currency, contrary to the popular image. However, after the establishment of Fort Orange in 1624, both the quantity and distribution of wampum increased, and it quickly became a medium of exchange. For discussions on the history, manufacture, and use of wampum refer to Lafitau (1974, 1977), Morgan (1962), Beauchamp (1901), Wray and Schoff (1953), Fenton (1971), Ceci (1977, 1982), and Tooker (1978).

A "hand" is a common European length measurement, equivalent to about four inches.

32. Duffel is a coarse woolen cloth with a thick nap and was an important and popular trade item.

Marten (*Martes americana*).

33. Individuals identified in the literature as "diviners," "clair-
voyants," and "fortune tellers," who were often shaman or medicine
men, and their activities and paraphenalia are discussed at length in
Lafitau (1974), Tooker (1964, pp. 83–87), Parker (1928), Shimony
(1961), Trigger (1976), and Herrick (1977). For additional information
see notes 74, 113, and 115.

The "idols" mentioned here refer to personal charms, a variety
of objects such as animal claws or skins regarded as having supernatural
power. They could function as witchcraft charms or bring the charm's
owner good luck in hunting, trading, and gambling (cf. Tooker 1964,
pp. 120–122; Shimony 1961, pp. 285–286).

Pigeon (Passenger pigeon, *Ectopistes migratorius,* extinct, or possibly
Mourning dove, *Zenaida macroura*).

34. *Sickaris* in modern Mohawk is *shikká:rus* 'while I am peeling
the bark off'. *Shi-* is a prepronominal prefix called the coincident, *-k-*
is the pronoun 'I', *-kar-* is the verb root 'to peel bark off', *-us* is the
serial aspect suffix. A name of this grammatical form is rather un-
common. These goods are standard European trade items made available to the Mohawk.

35. *Onekahoncka.* This is the name of the first settlement visited
by the Dutchmen.

Native speakers recognized only the noun root *-hnek-* 'water' or
'liquid' in this word and could provide no further information regarding its meaning.

36. *Canowarode.* This is the second settlement mentioned by Van
den Bogaert. It was not visited.

This word is *kanú:warote?* in modern Mohawk and means 'a nail
stuck into the wall'. It consists of the noun root *-nuwar-* 'nail', and the
verb root *-ot-* 'to be standing'.

The site of this village has not been precisely identified, although
its suspected location is approximately one and one-half miles east of
Randall (see map).

37. *Schatsyerosy.* This is the third village, comprised of 12 houses
and also apparently without a palisade. This word looks like *skatsi-
?eróhtsyu* 'one fingernail removed'. It contains the noun root *-tsi?er-*
plus the verb root *-ohtsy-* 'to remove'.

This site has not been identified archaeologically; however, it, like
the previous settlement, was probably near the river on the floodplain,
and is most likely located just west of *Canowarode* near Randall.

38. Archaeological research has established that Mohawk ceme-

teries, often two or three per village, were usually placed in proximity to a settlement (see note 85).

39. *Canagere.* This is identified as the second castle by Van den Bogaert, even though it is without a palisade.

This word may be *kaná:kareʔ* 'sticks'.

Recent archaeological excavations at the Rumrill-Naylor site near Sprakers appear to support a hypothesis that this was the village of *Canagere* visited by Van den Bogaert and his party.

40. As mentioned previously, many Iroquois villages were surrounded by a palisade or stockade (see note 66).

41. This observation, and the sentence following, indicate that at least in this village, the inhabitants had dispersed into the forests to hunt deer. Both men and women participated in this activity (Trigger 1976, p. 39; Fenton 1978, p. 298).

42. *Tonnosatton.* This word could be *thonuhsáhtu* 'he takes the whole house away'. It contains the noun root *-nuhs-* 'house' and the verb root *-ahtu-* 'to disappear'.

Toniwerot. This name may contain the noun root *-wer-* 'wind' or 'air'.

Both of these men are described as chiefs of the village of *Canagere.*

43. The original document reads *met sij eygen honden,* i.e., 'with his own dogs'. Although on December 12 there is a reference to dogs, it is doubtful that they would have been used to hunt beaver. Therefore, *honden* is assumed to be a copyist's error for *handen,* meaning 'hands'.

44. Beaver (*Castor canadensis*) were not only exploited for their pelts but were at the same time a food source, increasing in importance as trade and the requirements for pelts intensified (Grayson 1974; Lenig 1977, p. 73).

45. The keeping of bears in enclosures within a village appears to have been a common practice among Northern Iroquoians. Tooker (1964, p. 66) summarizes observations by Champlain and Sagard, noting that bears, probably cubs whose mothers had been killed (Trigger 1976, p. 41), might be fattened for two or three years and then butchered and eaten in celebration of a feast. The structures in which they were penned were, as Van den Bogaert describes, small log houses or round cagelike enclosures formed by driving stakes into the ground. Sagard (1968, p. 220) says that the bears were fed *sagamité,* a boiled corn soup, while Van den Bogaert states that the one he saw "ate everything given to it" (see note 79).

In general, bears were important animals to the Iroquois. They were not only a source of food and fur but occupied a prominent position in Iroquois ideology and religion. The Bear Society was and is an important medicine society in Iroquois communities and the Bear dance an integral part of the Midwinter Ceremony (cf. Tooker 1964; Fenton 1987).

46. Sulfur (S. Orthorhombic) appears to have been traded in, since the Mohawks say that they had obtained it from the "foreign Indians." It is likely that it had originated from Silurian evaporate beds located in the Buffalo-Rochester region of the state. Here, deposits of the Salina group, containing mostly dolomite, halite, and anhydrite, produce sulfur. The Salina group extends westward as far as Ohio; therefore, any part of this area may have been the source of sulfur (Robert J. Dineen, Richard W. Wiener, Geological Survey, New York State Museum and Science Service, personal communication, 1980).

That the sulfur was obtained from "foreign Indians" certainly suggests that it had not been acquired locally, and probably not from others of the Five Nations Iroquois. Instead, it may have been received in trade from the Erie, Wenro, or Neutral, Iroquoian speakers resident in western New York and Southern Ontario (White 1978a, 1978b; cf. JR, v. 43, pp. 259–61).

47. *Guilder*. A Dutch monetary unit. A day's work for a common laborer in New Netherland was worth one guilder.

48. It is interesting to note the presence of women on the trail without the escort of men and transporting items to trade, e.g., salmon and tobacco. Generally, it is suggested and assumed that only men traded (Tooker 1964, p. 58; Trigger 1976, pp. 62–65; Engelbrecht 1972, p. 8). Women may have begun to take a role in this activity following a general population decline and increased male deaths as a result of epidemics and warfare. However, perhaps women had always been involved at some level in trade and that their participation has simply gone unreported. These women are identified as "sinnekens," probably Oneida.

Salmon (Atlantic salmon, *Salmo salar*) could have been obtained from any number of water sources north and west of the Mohawk. These anadromous fish are known to have ascended the Oswego and Oneida rivers and numerous other tributaries to the St. Lawrence River and Lake Ontario. They were not present in the Mohawk (see also note 95).

49. This letter has never been located.

50. *Sqorhea.* This may be the Mohawk noun *oskóharaʔ* 'skeleton'.

51. Moving west from the fourth village, the only major stream encountered matching the description offered here is Canajoharie Creek (see map).

52. The location of this fifth settlement, the "third castle," has not been identified satisfactorily. It is probably situated in the area of Happy Hollow Road between present-day Canajoharie and Fort Plain (see map).

Schanidisse resembles *skanatísuʔ* 'the town has been remade'. This could be segmented as *s-* 'again', *-ka-* 'it', *-nat-* 'town', *-is-* 'to complete, finish', and *-u,* a stative suffix. It may be that *Schanidisse* was a recently established village and that Van den Bogaert's query as to what the village was called was misdirected by him or misunderstood by the Indians, so that he received the answer "the town has been remade." Fenton (1978, p. 302) notes that village removal "was a gradual process, one town going up while the other was decaying, as commemorated in the place-name theme: 'New Town' and 'Old Town'," and provides *kanadase:ʔ* (Seneca) 'newtown' (personal communication 1987).

Tewowary is possibly *tehóhareʔ* 'he has suspended something in two different places'. This word consists of the dualic prefix *te-,* the pronoun *-h-* 'he', the verb root *-ohar-* 'to suspend something', and the stative suffix *-eʔ.*

53. The "lion's skin" is likely that of a mountain lion (*Felis concolor*).

54. About seven species of oak (*Quercus*) are native to the Mohawk Valley. Butternuts (*Juglans cinerea*) and black walnuts (*Juglans nigra*) are also present, the former being abundant (Starna 1976).

55. Although not identified satisfactorily, this site is presumed to be one located on Prospect Hill in the village of Fort Plain (see map).

Osquage is probably pronounced *ohskwà:ke,* which is *ahskwà:ke* in modern Mohawk. This word means 'on top of the roof'. Native speakers pointed out that this kind of roof has no walls but only posts.

56. *Oquoho* is *okwáho* 'wolf'. This term is used either in connection with the animal or with a member of the Wolf Clan. Native speakers insisted that it cannot be used as a personal name. Thus, it appears that Van den Bogaert had been told of this chief's clan affiliation; that is, he is a member of the Wolf Clan, he is a wolf. The Mohawk have three clans, the Turtle, the Bear, and the Wolf (Fenton 1978; Tooker

1978). Iroquois clans are composed of two or more matrilineages and are fictive kin groups (Fenton 1978; Shimony 1961).

57. This large stream, west of *Osquage*, is in all likelihood Otsquago Creek at Fort Plain (see map).

58. *Minquas.* This is a reference to the Susquehannock, whom the Dutch call Minquas (Jennings 1978).

59. It is interesting to note that Van den Bogaert is asked to "heal a man who is very sick." A brief mention in Lafitau (1977, p. 215) supports the general supposition that additional individuals might be called in to assist ill persons if curing them was considered hopeless or interest in effecting a cure had diminished.

60. The seventh settlement, *Cawaoge*, was probably just west of Fort Plain (see map). *Cawaoge* could be *kahahò:ke* 'a place where the road is submerged'. There is the neuter pronoun *ka-* 'it', the noun root *-hah-* 'road', the verb root *-o-* 'be in the water', and the locative suffix *-ke*.

61. Savin trees are of the juniper family: the red cedar (*Juniperus virginica*), and the northern white cedar (*Thuya occidentalis*) (Starna 1976).

62. The eighth village may have been on the south side of the Mohawk River just west of the mouth of Caroga Creek, a tributary on the north side. Evidence of structures which may be those mentioned by Van den Bogaert as being used for grain storage has been found near the creek's mouth (Donald Lenig, personal communication 1976). The site of *Tenotoge* was probably destroyed by the construction of the New York State Thruway.

Tenotoge is *teyonutó:kv* 'between two mountains' or 'valley'. It contains the dualic prefix *te-*, the neuter pronoun *-yo-* 'it', the noun root *-nut-* 'mountain', and the verb root *-okv* 'two things forking or merging'.

63. The course of the Mohawk River in this vicinity strongly supports the suspected geographic location of *Tenotoge* mentioned in the previous note (see map).

64. Archaeological research has uncovered evidence suggesting the form of structures that may have functioned as granaries or other forms of storage (Tuck 1971; Ritchie and Funk 1973). For the most part, such structures were very much like longhouses; however, interior sleeping platforms and other features generally associated with a domicile are absent (Starna 1980, p. 374). At the early Howlett Hill site in the Onondaga area, a small circular structure attached to a house has been interpreted as a granary (Tuck 1971, p. 85).

65. Unlike *Canagere*, this village is fully populated (see note 41). There is the possibility that the residents of each village hunted at different times during the winter so that one village might have been nearly abandoned, its population dispersed in hunting parties, while at another, people might have been at home. It is also possible that the residents of *Tenotoge* had very recently returned from the winter hunt.

66. The deteriorated condition of what had been a triple palisade around this village suggests that it had been occupied for many years (Sykes 1980; Starna 1980). A move to a new village may have been imminent.

The form and technique of construction of palisades among Northern Iroquoians are discussed by Pendergast (1979), Abler (1970), Ritchie and Funk (1973), and Tuck (1971). Generally, there were two or three rows of posts or timbers, anchored or driven into the ground, surrounding a village. The outer and inner rows were often angled toward each other and secured at the top. Bark boards and saplings were interlaced among the uprights, reinforcing them and forming a virtually impenetrable wall 12 to 20 feet in height. There were platforms for warriors placed near the top of the wall which were reached by ladders.

67. This description of Mohawk armament and armor corresponds well with that of other Iroquoian groups where twined reed armor or a cuirass covering the chest, arms, and legs, along with a skin shield and leather cap, were worn. Weapons included the bow and arrow, and ball-headed war clubs (cf. JR, v. 24, p. 205; Tooker 1964, p. 30); Trigger 1976, pp. 70, 196–97, 252; Lafitau 1977, pp. 115–16, plate VIII; Fenton 1978, p. 316). Note the apparent absence of guns (see note 69).

68. "The northern Iroquoians and their Algonquian neighbors were head hunters from the earliest times" (Fenton 1978, p. 316). For a history of scalping and other forms of obtaining war trophies, see Axtell and Sturtevant (1980). Killing and scalping were not the prime directives of the Iroquois in warfare. Instead, the preferred alternative was to take prisoners and return them for adoption.

69. This is the first of four instances where the Dutchmen are asked to fire their pistols. The obvious curiosity of the Mohawk expressed here and elsewhere in the journal suggests strongly that they had not yet been able to acquire firearms for themselves. Indeed, the literature shows that the Mohawk did not obtain guns until about 1640

(Fenton 1978, p. 316; Trigger 1976, pp. 630–32; Hunt 1940, pp. 166–69). By 1642, however, the situation had so changed that Arent van Curler and his party were "saluted . . . with divers musket-shots" upon their approach to a Mohawk village (O'Callaghan 1846, p. 463).

70. Beans, mentioned several times in the journal, were an important domesticate among the Iroquois. A great number of varieties was grown (Waugh 1916; Parker 1910). They formed one part of the triad of corn, beans, and squash, the "Three Sisters" (Fenton 1978, p. 299). Evidence for these principal crops first appears in the archaeological record about A.D. 1000. Other cultivated plants include the sunflower and tobacco.

Wild strawberries (*Fragaria vesca americana* and *Fragaria virginiana*). These fruits are of considerable significance to the Iroquois and are celebrated in the calendric round of thanksgiving ceremonies. Today, as in the past, the purpose of the Strawberry Ceremony includes giving thanks for the first fruits of the new season and to entertain the food spirits to assure continued good harvests (Shimony 1961, p. 159; Morgan 1962, pp. 197–98).

71. Chestnuts (American chestnut, *Castanea dentata*); blueberries (*Vaccinium*), about eight native species; and sunflower seeds from the sunflower plant (*Helianthus*) of which there are six native species (Starna 1976).

72. According to Van den Bogaert's word list (see Wordlist, p. 61), *Sunachkoes* or *sinachkoo* means "(to) exorcise the devil." The modern form *hatsináhkv* 'exorcist' was known to one informant in Kahnawake, who said that it was used on the Six Nations Reserve in Ontario. Eight or nine years before Van den Bogaert heard it among the Mohawk, Nicolaes van Wassenaer recorded *Koutsinacka* 'devil hunter' [1626] (Jameson 1909, pp. 68, 87). Also, the Jesuit missionary Jacques Bruyas, who did his linguistic fieldwork in the Mohawk country in the 1670s, also came across this term, which he listed as *Atsinnachen* 'jongleur' (Bruyas 1863, p. 43). In his writings on shamanism Lafitau (1974, p. 237) lists the word *agotsinnachen* 'seers'. All of these Mohawk forms contain the verb root *-tsin-* 'to be energetic'.

Shaman or medicine men were part-time magico-religious specialists who interacted with supernaturals on behalf of themselves or individual clients. They derived their magical and curative powers from supernatural sources and were the performers in public and private rituals where curing and divination took place (cf. Tooker 1964, p. 91ff.).

73. *Ell.* An ell is a standard of measurement equal to 27 inches.

74. The shamanistic or curing rituals described by Van den Bogaert (see also entry for January 4) are some of the most detailed found in the literature. Refer to discussions on shamanism, illness, curing, and medicine in Lafitau (1974), Parker (1928), Fenton (1941, 1942a, 1987), Shimony (1961), Tooker (1964), Trigger (1976), and Herrick (1977).

Absolute identification of the specific medicine societies participating in the curing rituals as depicted in the journal is difficult to determine. In this case, *rona:kon?s* (Mohawk), *hona:tko?s* (Cayuga), powerful medicine men, are the actors. These men are "capable of casting evil spells or sickness on anyone at will, or [they may] break any of [the] evil spells or sickness cast on anybody. Their power sources usually come from charms they . . . possess . . . anything from bones, skins, stones, or some herbs. These bones could come from animals, but the biggest power seems to come from human bones. To break these spells we speak of . . . we often [do this] by inducing vomiting for the victim or dancing songs of the devil" (Reginald Henry, Cayuga Faithkeeper, personal communication, 1981).

75. Again, the Mohawk ask the Dutchmen to fire their weapons. *Allese rondade* or *Alle sarondade* (see entry of January 12) is *á:re sarú:tat* 'fire again!' in modern Mohawk. *á:re* means 'again', and the verb root *-aru?tat-* means 'to blow' or 'to shoot'. Compare *arontaton 'souffler'* (Bruyas 1863, p. 26).

76. There are three species of birch native to the Mohawk Valley *Betula alba papyrifera, B. alleghaniensis, B. populifolia* (Starna 1976).

77. Elk (*Cervus canadensis*) were once found in the region.

78. Beech trees (*Fagus grandifolia*) (Starna 1976).

79. *Sappaen.* This a variant form of *samp* (Narragansett *nasaump*), meaning corn soup or mush. The French called it *sagamité* (Waugh 1916, pp. 91–93).

80. After leaving *Tenotoge,* Van den Bogaert and his companions appear to have traveled overland in a nearly westerly direction. There is no evidence in the journal to suggest that they continued to follow the Mohawk River. Instead, it is more likely that they passed south of the river in as direct a route as possible to the Oneida village (see map). His observations of going "over hills and through thickets" in walking through woods of oak, birch, and beech support this contention. Their destination was *Onneyuttehage (Onvyote?á:ka)* 'the people of the place of the standing stone' (see note 99), the Oneida. Some villages

of the Oneida have been identified archaeologically, clustering in the southeast section of present-day Madison County (Pratt 1976, p. 171, figure 5).

81. It is impossible to identify the streams that Van den Bogaert was crossing. That they "flowed" in the direction he describes may be an error or a misunderstanding of his Indian guides (note 8 makes reference to his difficulties with directional prepositions). Streams that he and his party encountered might have been tributaries of the Mohawk, therefore flowing north. The Indians may have said, for example, that following the streams south would eventually lead him to that river which flowed into the Minquas' country, the Susquehanna, or to the South River, the Delaware. On the other hand, since his route to the Oneida may have run along the divide between the Mohawk and Susquehanna watersheds, it is possible that he crossed the headwaters of several south-flowing waterways, e.g., North Winfield Creek and the West Branch of the Unadilla (see map).

82. River otter (*Lutra canadensis*).

83. The generic term "ironwood" refers to the hop hornbeam (*Carpinus caroliniana*) or the American hornbeam (*Ostrya virginiana*), although it is likely that Van den Bogaert saw the latter since this species is generally found in the same environmental niche as oak.

84. Here the Indians are pointing out the Mohawk River to Van den Bogaert from a high vantage near the Oneida village. Their location at this time was probably on one of several high hills some 20 miles south of the river (see map) where such a view would have been possible. Note that on the previous day (December 29), Van den Bogaert writes of coming to "a very high hill."

85. Van den Bogaert's observations here agree with other descriptions of graves and burial practices among Northern Iroquoians found in Lafitau (1977, pp. 231–35), Morgan (1962, pp. 172–73), Tooker (1964, p. 130), Trigger (1976, pp. 52–53), Champlain (1967, pp. 245–46), and Van der Donck (1968, pp. 86–88).

The body of a dead person was placed in a flexed position, with the legs drawn up to the chest and the arms arranged so that the hands were near or covering the face. The corpse was bound tightly in a fur robe or skins and placed in a grave which was usually lined with bark or mats. Goods such as food, weapons, tools, etc., were often placed in the grave to accompany the soul of the dead person on its final journey.

86. The high ground mentioned is the scarp of the Tug Hill Plateau (Fenneman 1938).

87. This is a reference to Oneida Lake, about 18 to 20 miles north-northwest from the Oneida village. The French entered the lake via the Oswego and Oneida rivers (see map). It also can be seen from some of the vantage points mentioned in note 84.

88. The form of greeting given Van den Bogaert and his party is typical Iroquois protocol that is carried out at the "wood's edge." This is the literal and symbolic junction between the "clearing" (the village and adjacent fields), the domain of the women, and the "forest" the domain of the men (cf. Fenton 1978; Tooker 1978, 1984; Hamell 1981). Similar examples of such greetings are recorded in the early documents.

89. Pratt (1976, p. 136) states that the Thurston site is probably the village visited by Van den Bogaert in 1634–1635. This conclusion is based on limited knowledge of the village settlement pattern and a snuff box dated to 1634, along with several musket balls, recovered during archaeological excavations. Pratt suggests that the latter items may be those fired by Van den Bogaert to celebrate the New Year (see journal entry, December 31). Our position is that more investigation and data gathering are necessary to firmly establish which of the known Oneida sites of the period is actually that visited by the Dutchmen.

90. There are few references regarding the details of aesthetic, decorative, or otherwise symbolic elements or motifs on Iroquois longhouses. Lafitau (1977, p. 20) mentions that houses were decorated on the inside, while Morgan (1962, p. 318) says that over one of the two entrances to a longhouse was "cut the tribal device of the head of the family." The conclusion drawn here is that Van den Bogaert had seen gables painted with totemic animal figures depicting the clan of the women of the household.

91. Note 19 describes longhouse construction, including the raised sleeping platforms mentioned here.

92. The councillor referred to here may be a sachem or a village chief (see note 26).

93. Van den Bogaert is being chastised for not having participated in a form of social behavior fundamental not only to the Iroquois but to other cultures as well. This is reciprocity, an underlying principle governing social interaction whereby obligations are incurred and met,

often taking the form of gift giving or exchange. Such exchange functioned to form and maintain social and economic alliances and networks.

94. The river is the Oswego and/or the Oneida, connecting Lake Ontario and Oneida Lake (see map).

95. Salmon and other fish were taken in a number of ways by Northern Iroquoians including the use of weirs, gill nets, seines, and spears (Beauchamp 1905, pp. 130–31, 147–48; Heidenreich 1971, pp. 208–212). Although fish are available throughout the year, the peak fishing season was in the spring, i.e., March through May, when large numbers of fish ascended rivers and their tributaries to spawn. Waugh (1916, p. 136) discusses briefly fish as a food resource among the Iroquois (see note 48).

96. *Jawe Arenias* is *nyá:wv* 'Thank you', Arenias! One informant suggested that this name be analyzed as *arénye?s* 'he spreads himself', 'he is a charismatic person', with *-areny-* 'to spread', and the habitual suffix *-e?s.*

97. It is unlikely that there were people with horns living in the Tug Hill Plateau region at this or any other time. By making such a claim, however, the Indians were doubtlessly attempting to frighten the Dutchmen, discouraging them from exploring the region, and thereby preventing expansion of trade. Such an expansion would have eroded a middleman position already held or anticipated by some of the Five Nations Iroquois.

98. From 1582 until the Dutch surrendered New Amsterdam to the English in 1664, the Gregorian calendar or "New Style" was in use by most of the United Provinces of the Netherlands (Stokes 1967, v. 4, p. 24). This system replaced the "Old Style" or Julian calendar, adjusting for the 10 days by which the vernal equinox had become displaced and introducing "leap years" to maintain this correction.

99. *Onneyuttehage* is *onvyote?á:ka,* 'the people of the standing stone', the Oneida, the Iroquois group located immediately west of the Mohawks (cf. Campisi 1978). This Mohawk term consists of the noun prefix *o-* 'it', the noun root *-nvy-* 'stone', the verb root *-ot-* 'to be standing', the aspect suffix *-e?-,* and the populative *-(h)aka* 'people'.

100. *Ho* or *Jo.* In old Huron "*ho, ho, ho*" was a "salutation of joy" (Sagard 1968, p. 85). In modern Mohawk *yó:* is an expression of approval of what someone else has just said.

Schene I Atsiehoene may very well be *skv́:nv vtyóhawe?* 'Peace it will bring forth'. *skv́:nv* is 'peace', *v-* is the future prefix 'will', *-t-* is the cislocative prefix, in this case meaning 'forth', *-yo-* is the pronoun 'it', *-haw-* is the verb root 'to hold', and *-e ʔ* is the aspect suffix.

101. *Netho* is *ta ʔné ʔtho ʔ* 'so be it!' in modern Mohawk. Compare *etho* 'response of approbation' (Lafitau 1974, p. 298), and *etho* 'oui, bien!' (Cuoq 1882, p. 4).

102. *Katon* is *kátu ʔ* 'let us consent' in modern Mohawk.

103. *Hÿ.* This is obviously another expression of approval. *Hai* 'hail' occurs in modern Condolence Council chants (Tooker 1978).

104. *Onnedaeges.* This is *onutà:ke* 'on the hill', a reference to the Onondaga, an Iroquois group west of the Oneida located southeast of present-day Syracuse (cf. Blau, Campisi, and Tooker 1978).

105. "Castle" appears to be a term the Dutchmen are applying to the tribe or nation of the Onondaga, although they could also be referring to a fortified village.

106. "Long cloth" is duffel (see note 32).

107. The translation here is from Dutch to Onondaga through an intermediary. Although related, the Northern Iroquoian languages spoken by the Five Nations Iroquois are and were, to a degree, mutually unintelligible. The most closely related, Mohawk and Oneida, are nearly mutually comprehensible with effort, but Onondaga is sufficiently different as to require translation (cf. Feister 1978).

108. *Manhatas.* Manhattan, New Amsterdam.

109. Wouter van Twiller, director of New Netherland from 1633 to 1638; nephew of Kiliaen van Rensselaer (see Introduction).

110. *Welsmachkoo.* It is not clear whether the accompanying quotation contains a translation of this word or whether *Welsmachkoo* is only an opening remark which was not translated.

There is little doubt that the first two letters, *we-*, constitute a prepronominal prefix, the factual, which in Mohawk generally points to a single event in the immediate past. The letters *-sma-* could be read as *-s(e)wa-*, the pronominal prefix 'you all'. As to the verb base, there is in Mohawk a verb root *-kw-* meaning 'to pick something up from the ground'. The root *-kw-* has an alternate shape *-ko-*, followed by the glottal stop *ʔ*, in the punctual aspect. *Welsmachkoo* could thus be analyzed as *wesewá:ko ʔ* 'you all picked up'.

There is another possibility. The last syllable in *Welsmachkoo* could be the verb *-kv-* 'to see' in the punctual aspect. The result would be *wesewá:kv ʔ* 'you all saw it'.

A good case could also be made that *Welsmachkoo* is *wesanà:khwv ʔ* 'you got angry' in modern Mohawk. Such a rendering appears quite plausible if Van den Bogaert's entry of January 1 is examined. There it says: "An Indian once again called us scoundrels, as has been previously told, and he was very malicious so that Willem Tomassen became so angry that the tears ran from his eyes." The segments of *wesanà:khwv* are the factual prefix *we-*, the objective pronoun *-sa-*, the verb root *-na*ʔ*khwv-* 'to get angry', and the punctual aspect suffix *ʔ*.

111. HA ASSIRONI ATSIMACHKOO KENT OYAKAYING WEE ONNEYATTE ONAONDAGE KOYOCKWE HOO SENOTO WANYAGWEGANNE HOO SCHENE-HALATON KASTEN KANOSONI YNDICKO. In this passage is the first separate listing of the five Iroquois tribes in a contemporary record. Also found here may be the earliest known reference to the League of the Iroquois or the Iroquois Confederacy—KANOSONI.

There are two terms for the Iroquois League: one is *kanuhsú:ni* 'the built house', and the other is *kanuhsyú:ni* 'the extended house'. The latter form appears to be older and more common than the former (cf. Bruyas 1863, p. 18; Hodge 1907, pp. 617, 620; Ives Goddard's synonymy in Fenton 1978, p. 320). It is not known which form Van den Bogaert actually heard at Oneida. It may have been either *kanuhsú:ni* or *kanuhsyú:ni*, which in phonetic rendering is *gunūhsú:ni* and *gunūhsū̃:ni* respectively. If he had heard the form *kanushyú:ni*, there is no doubt that the Indians were referring to the Iroquois League. On the other hand, if it was *kanuhsú:ni* the Indians may have just told him that a house would be built. However, given the context and what Van den Bogaert understood regarding what the Indians had told him, we feel certain that the reference was to the League. Following this passage, Van den Bogaert notes that among other things, "I would have a house and fire, wood and anything else." He does not indicate that anyone would build him a house, but instead, he appears to be saying that he would simply be provided shelter and amenities. However, since the one form is the accepted term for the Iroquois League, while the other could possibly refer to it, there is the strong possibility that this is the earliest record of the League's existence.

As to the other parts of the passage, the first two words refer to white men. The third word *atsimachkoo* appears to contain the verb root *-tsinahk(w)-* or possibly *-tsina-* plus a suffix. Modern Mohawk has a word *ratsí:na*ʔ 'he is a daring fellow'. If this form is followed by the interrogative particle *kv*, the result is *ratsí:na*ʔ*kv* 'is he a daring fellow?'

It is also possible to analyze *atsimachkoo* as *ratsináhkv* 'sorcerer' or 'doctor'. Thus, the possible choices are "is the white man a daring fellow?" or "the white man is a sorcerer." In context either one of these translations is appropriate. However, Van den Bogaert, a barber-surgeon, had been asked early in his journey to attend to someone who was ill. The Indians may therefore have referred to him as a white man who was a doctor. There is little doubt that *-kaying wee* (from OYAKAYING WEE) is *kanyṽ:ke* 'Mohawk'. Megapolensis (1909, p. 172), writing ten years later, provides *Kajingahaga* 'Mohawk people'. Also, since Van den Bogaert lists the Iroquois tribes from east to west, the word *kaying wee* correctly precedes the word *onneyatte* 'Oneida', situated adjacent to the Mohawk.

Finally, it is tempting to equate the last word in this passage, *yndicko*, with *judicha* 'conflagration', found in the wordlist; however, this would be somewhat tenuous. Consequently, a blank is left there.

A possible rendering of the passage is as follows:

HA ASSIRONI	ATSIMACHKOO	KENT	O/YA/KAYING WEE
ra ?serú:ni	*ratsí:na ?kʋ*	*kṽ:tho*	*ká:yʋ kanyṽ:ke*
	ratsináhkʋ		
The white man	is he a daring fellow?	here	it is Mohawk
	is a sorcerer/doctor		

ONNEYATTE	ONAONDAGE	KOYOCKWE	HOO SENOTO	WANY/AGWEGAN/NE HOO
onṽ:yote ?	*onutà:ke*	*koyó:kwʋ*	*hotinutó:wane ?*	*thiwakwé:ku*
Oneida	Onondaga	Cayuga	Seneca	all over

SCHENE/HALTON	KASTEN	KANOSONI	YNDICKO
skṽ:nʋ horá:tu	*kástha ?*	*kanuhsyú:ni*	
safely he is lying down	it is useful	Iroquois League	

The gloss of this passage is obviously disjointed and undoubtedly represents only a fragment of what was a much longer statement by the Indians.

The significance of this passage has not been previously recognized. Certainly, General Wilson, the original translator, was not aware of its meaning in Mohawk, choosing only to translate Van den Bogaert's Dutch. Soon after the journal's initial publication, Beauchamp (1895, p. 322) noted that the passage contained the names of the Iroquois' "castles", *Onneyatte, Onaondage, Koyockure,* and "the two Seneca castles of Honotowany and Senenehalaton, apparently forms of Souontouane and Tiotohaton." He was not only inaccurate in the translation, but he was unaware of a transcription error committed by Wilson. In the original Wilson (1896, p. 95) transcribed the word "Kanosoni" as "Franosoni," which is not a Mohawk sound sequence (cf. Jameson 1909, p. 152). For more on the League, consult Tooker (1978).

112. The system of etiquette observed by Van den Bogaert conforms generally to that described by Morgan (1962, p. 327ff.) and Tooker (1978, p. 57).

113. Turtle shell rattles are used to accompany singers and dancers in Iroquois ritual and ceremony (Fenton 1942b, 1987), and form part of the paraphernalia used by medicine men and shaman. They are most often made from the shells of snapping turtles (*Chelydra serpentina*) and box turtles (*Terrapene carolina*) (Ritchie 1969, p. 118).

114. Bunches of corn were hung from the rafters of longhouses as part of food storage technology. The corn was struck at during the curing ritual, dislodging accumulated dust.

115. As mentioned in note 74, clear identification of the medicine societies participating in the curing ritual is problematical. It is possible that the ritual here is being performed by the "Medicine Company" or "Society of Shamans," the *hadii?dos* or *yei?dos* (Seneca) (Kurath 1964, p. 11–12). Such a ritual is usually held at night and in secret in the patient's home. It involves several marching songs sung by a company of twelve to fifteen men shaking gourd rattles.

Sucking as part of a curative procedure is a widespread practice among North American Indians. "The Iroquois also hold that witchcraft charms [causing illness] may be extracted from the patient by giving an emetic or by sucking" (Tooker 1964, p. 117).

It may be that the otter skin was the personal charm of the sick person or one of the curers, functioning to neutralize the evilness that had been removed through sucking (cf. Fenton 1987).

116. This stone is presumably chert, or commonly, flint.

117. This letter has never been located.

118. *Sinck.* A Sinneken (see note 1).

119. *Onnedagens.* The Onondaga (see note 104).

120. *Canastogeera.* This means 'white rafter'. It contains the Onondaga noun root -*nast*- 'rafter' and the verb root -*k[ę]Rata*- 'white' (Hanni Woodbury, personal communication, 1987).

121. This is Onondaga Lake which the French could have reached via the Oswego and Oneida rivers.

122. See note 75.

123. This may be a reference to either the Delaware or the Susquehanna River and the European settlements there.

124. *Satteeu* is sateen, an English name for a cotton fabric used for linings.

125. Hares (*Lepus*), or cottontails (*Sylvilagus*).

126. Wampum was distributed to bereaved individuals to condole a death (Tooker 1978, p. 423).

127. See note 62.

128. See note 60.

129. See note 55.

130. See note 56.

131. *Aromyas* is *Arenias*; see note 96.

132. See note 52.

133. *Taturot.* In modern Mohawk this would be *thothú:rote?* 'he has a gun standing at his side'. It contains the noun root -*hur*- 'blowgun' and the verb root -*ot*- 'to be standing'.

134. This letter has never been located.

135. The site of this village has not been identified.

The Mohawk-Mahican wars (1624–1628) are detailed in Trigger (1971) and Brasser (1978b).

Mahicanders. The Mahican (Brasser 1978b).

WORDLIST

HE FOLLOWING WORDLIST, found at the end of Van den Bogaert's journal, is the earliest known philological treatment of the Mohawk language in existence. Its author deserves high praise for recording a vocabulary of such quality, especially considering the conditions under which the list was made and the fact that he was interacting with people who spoke a language that was utterly exotic when compared to his own.

The wordlist is arranged as follows: The left-hand column provides Van den Bogaert's rendering of the Mohawk language as he heard and recorded it, while the column on the right contains the transcription of the Dutch equivalent, followed by an English gloss. These data were provided by Charles T. Gehring and William A. Starna, editors of this volume. On the next line, and in brackets, I have furnished the modern Mohawk equivalent with an English gloss, where possible.

As the reader will note, there are a number of words which could not be identified by native speakers of Mohawk. Also, it is obvious that Van den Bogaert's queries about language did not always elicit the desired response. For example, at some point he asked a question aimed at learning the word or phrase for "immediately." The answer was "not yet." It is not surprising that the manner of asking a question about an object or concept would, at times, cause confusion, both on the Dutchman's part

51

and that of the Indians. Where appropriate, I have made observations regarding some of these difficulties.

The letter "v" represents a nasal vowel comparable to the *on* in French *maison*, the symbol "ʔ" represents a glottal stop, ":" is vowel length, "´" is a rising tone, and "`" is a falling one.

I wish to express my gratitude to Mike Norton, Catherine Norton, and Frank Natawe, of Kahnawake, Quebec, for their expert help in identifying Mohawk words and phrases.

GUNTHER MICHELSON

Maquase spraeck [Mohawk language]	Nederlanse spraeck [Dutch language]	
assire oft oggaha [*áhsire*ʔ 'blanket'] [*okúha*ʔ] 'felt' (material)	duffels laecken	'cloth'
atoga [*ató:kv*ʔ 'axe']	Byllen	'axes'
atsochta [*atsò:ktv*ʔ 'hoe']	dissels	'adzes'
assere [*à:share*ʔ 'knife']	messen	'knives'
assaghe [*áhsikwe*ʔ 'spear']	rappie(r) lennet	'rapier'
attochwat [*atókwa*ʔ 'spoon']	leepels	'spoons'
ondach [*ú:tak* 'kettle']	ceetels	'kettles'
endathatst [*yutatkvhstha*ʔ 'mirror']	spyegels	'looking glass'
tasaskarisat [*tewata*ʔ*shari:sas* 'scissors']	schaeren	'scissors'
kamrewari [*kanú:ware*ʔ 'awls'] [*karú:ware*ʔ 'awls']	Elsen ysers	'awls'
onekoera [*o*ʔ*nekórha*ʔ 'wampum']	sewant haer geldt	'sewan, their money'

tiggeretait	cammen	'combs'
[*atkerothí:ha?* 'comb']		
catse	Bellen	'bell'
[*kátshe?* 'jar']		
Dedaia Witha	hemden ofte	'shirts or
[*atyà:tawi* 'shirt', 'jacket']	rocken	coats'
nonnewarory	karpoesen mussen	'fur cap'
[*anù:warore?* 'hat']		
Eytroghe	craelen	'beads'
[*ohstarò:kwa?* 'large beads']		
Canagoesat	Schraepers	'scraper'
[*ohnakúhsa?* 'deer hide']¹		
Caris	Cousen	'stocking'
[*ká:ris* 'stockings']		
achta	schoenen	'shoes'
[*áhta?* 'shoe']		

Naemen van beesten soo daer vallen
[Names of animals found there]

aque	harten	'deer'²
aquesados	paerden	'horses'
[*akohsá:tvs* 'horse']		
adiron	katten	'cats'
[*atì:ru* 'raccoon']³		
aquidagon	Juck hoorn	'oxen'⁴
senotowanne	Elant	'elk'
[*oskenutó:wane?* 'elk']		
ochquari	Beeren	'bear'
[*ohkwá:ri?* 'bear']		
sinite	bever	'beaver'
[*tsyaní:to* 'beaver']		
tawyne	otter	'otter'
[*tawí:ne* 'otter']		
eyo	Minck	'mink'
[*ayó:ha?* 'mink']		
senadondo	vos	'fox'⁵
ochquoha	wolf	'wolf'
[*okwáho?* 'wolf']		
seranda	Mater	'marten'⁶

Ichar *or* sateeni
  [*è:rhar* 'dog']
  [*satshé:nv?* 'your domestic
  animal']
	hondt	'dog'

tali	kraen	'crane'[7]
kragequa	swaen	'swan'
kahanckt [*káhuk* 'wild goose']	gans	'geese'
schawariwane [*skaweró:wane?* 'turkey']	kallekoen	'turkey'
schascariwanasi	Arent	'eagle'
tantanege [*tauhtané:kv* 'rabbit']	haes	'hare'
onckwe [*ú:kwe* 'human being']	mensen	'men'
etsi [*rà:tsin* 'a male animal']	een man	'a man'

coenheckti
  [*o?nhétyv* 'a female
  animal']
	een vrou	'a woman'

ochtaha [*rokstúha* 'an old man']	een oudt man	'an old man'
odasqueta	een oude vrou	'an old woman'[8]

sine gechtera
  [*senekúhteru* 'you are a
  young man']
	een vryer	'a young
		man'

exhechta [*eksà:?a* 'a girl']	een vryster	'a young girl'
ragina [*ráke?ni* 'father!']	een vader	'father'
distan [*istv:?a* 'mother']	een moeder	'mother'
Cian [*riyv:?a* 'my son']	een Kint	'child'
rocksongwa [*raksà:?a* 'a boy']	een jongen	'boy'

cannawarori
  [*yonuhwaró:ri* 'she has
  loose morals']
	een hoer	'prostitute'

Onentar [*onuhtè:ra?* 'a support']⁹	een swaere vrou	'woman in labor', 'pregnant woman'
ragenonou [*rakenohà:?a* 'my uncle']	Oom	'uncle'
rackesie [*raktsì:?a* 'my older brother']¹⁰	Cousyn	'cousin'
anochquis [*onúhkwis* 'hair']	het haeyr	'hair'
anonsi [*onú:tsi* 'head']	het hooft	'head'
ochochta [*ohúhta?* 'ear']	de oren	'ears'
ohonckwa [*ohù:kwa?* 'throat'] [*onyà:kwa?* 'throat']	de keel	'throat'
oneyatsa [*o?nyúhsa?* 'nose']	de nues	'nose'
owanisse [*awv?náhsu* 'its tongue']	de tongh	'tongue'
onawy [*onawí:ra?* 'tooth']	de tanden	'teeth'
onenta [*onútsha?* 'arm']	de nermen	'arms'
osnotsa [*osnúhsa?* 'hand']	de handen	'hands'
onatassa	de vingeren	'fingers'
otichkera	den duyem	'thumb'
otsira [*otsi?é:ra?* 'fingernail']	de naegelen	'nails'
onirare [*onerà:rha?* 'shoulder blade']	het schouder blaedt	'shoulder blade'
orochquine [*oruhkwé:na?* 'spine']	het rugge been	'spine'
ossidau [*ohsì:ta?* 'foot']	de voeten	'feet'

onera	vroulyckheyt	'vagina'
[*yené:ru* 'she is pregnant']		
oeuda	Menschen dreck	'excrement'
[*óʔtaʔ* 'excrement']		
onsaha	de blaes	'bladder'
canderes	mandelyckheyt	'phallus'[11]
awasta	de klooten	'testicles'
casoya	een schip schuyt & kanoo	'ship' and 'canoe'
canossade	een huys ofte hutte	'house' or 'hut'
[*kanúhsoteʔ* 'there is a house']		
onega	waeter	'water'
[*ohné:kaʔ* 'a liquid']		
oetseira	vier	'fire'
[*ó:tsireʔ* 'fire']		
oyente	hout brant hout	'wood', 'firewood'
[*ó:yvteʔ* 'wood']		
osconte	bast van boomen	'bark'
[*oskú:taraʔ* 'sheet of bark']		
canadera	broodt	'bread'
[*kanà:taro* 'bread']		
ceheda	boonen	'beans'
[*osahè:taʔ* 'beans']		
oneste	Mayeys	'maize'
[*ó:nvhsteʔ* 'corn']		
cinsie	vis	'fish'
[*kútsyuʔ* 'fish']		
Ghekeront	sallem	'salmon'
[*kaké:ru* 'they lie on the ground'][12]		
oware	vlees	'meat'
[*oʔwà:ruʔ* 'meat']		
athesera	meel	'flour'
[*othè:seraʔ* 'flour']		
satsori	eeten	'to eat'
[*satshó:ri* 'slurp!']		
onighira	drincken	'to drink'
[*vkhnekí:raʔ* 'I shall drink']		

Kattenkerreyager   grooten honger   'very
[*vkatuhkárya?ke?* 'I shall be   hungry'
hungry']
augustuske   heel kout   'very cold'
[*vkewístoske?* 'I get cold']
oyendere   heel goedt   'very good'
[*yoyánere* 'it is good']
rockste   vriendt vrienden   'friends'
jachteyendere   ten duecht niet   'tis no good'
[*yáhte yoyánere* 'it is not
good']
quane   Groot   'large'
[*kowá:nv* 'large']
canyewa   kleyn   'small'
[*kv?niwà:?a* 'it is small']
wotstaha   Breet   'broad'
cates   dick   'thick'
[*kà:tvs* 'it is thick']
satewa   alleens   'alone'
[*sha?té:wa* 'it is of the
same size']¹³
sagat   dubbelt   'doubly'
[*neshá:kat* 'the same' (two
things)]
Awaheya   doot   'death'
[*yawvhé:yu* 'she is dead']
aghihi   sieck   'sick'
[*akíheye?* 'I could die']
sastorum   haest u wat   'hurry up'
[*satsnó:rat* 'hurry up!']
archoo   daetelyck   'immediately'
[*á:rekho* 'not yet']
owaetsei   neu   'now'
[*uwà:stsi* 'á little while
ago']
thederri   Gisteren   'yesterday'
[*thetú:re* 'yesterday']
Jorhani   morgen   'tomorrow'
[*vyórhv?ne?* 'tomorrow']

careyago	de lucht	'the light'
[*karuhyà:ke* 'in the sky']		
karackwero	de sonne	'the sun'
[*karáhkwa?* 'sun']		
Asistock	de sterren	'the stars'
[*otsíhsto?* 'star']		
sintho	saeyen	'(to) plant'
[*tsyútho* 'sow!']		
deserentekar	weyden	'(to) graze'
sorsar	Aen hoogen	'to raise'
Cana	saet	'seed'
[*kà:nv* 'seed']		
onea	steen	'stone'
[*onú:ya?* 'stone']		
Canadack *or* Cany	een sack oft mant	'sack or
[*kahnà:ta?* 'purse']		basket'
Canadaghi	een Casteel	'a castle'
[*kanatà:ke* 'in the village']		
oÿoghi	een Kill	'a waterway'
[*kayúha?* 'creek']		
canaderage	een revier	'a river'
[*kanyatarà:ke* 'on the lake']		
Johati	een padt oft wegh	'a path or
[*tyohá:te?* 'there is a path']		road'
onstara	huylen	'cry'
[*yutstárha?* 'they weep']		
aquayesse	lachen	'laugh'
[*yukwayéshu* 'we are		
chuckling']		
ohonte	Groente gras	'greens',
[*óhute?* 'grass']		'grass'
oneggeri	riet oft stroey	'reed' or
[*onékeri* 'hay']		'straw'
Christittye	yser cooper loot	'iron',
[*karístatsi* 'iron']		'copper',
		'lead'
onegonsera	roode verve	'red paint'
[*onekwúhtara?* 'red']14		
cahonsye	swart	'black'
[*kahù:tsi* 'black']		

Crage [*karà:kʋ* 'white']	witt	'white'
ossivenda [*otyarʋ̀:ta* 'orange-colored']	blau	'blue'
endatcondere [*okúhtshera?* 'the paint']	schildren	'(to) paint'
Joddireyo [*yuterí:yos* 'they fight']	vechten	'(to) fight'
Aquinachoo [*aukenà:khwʋ?* 'I would get angry']	Quaet	'angry'
Jaghacteroene [*yakohterù:ni* 'she is afraid']	vervaert	'afraid'
dadeneye [*tʋtení:yʋ* 'I bet you']	speelen dubbelen	'to gamble'
asserie [*ahserí:ye?* 'a rope']¹⁵	heel sterck	'very strong'
carente [*wakahrʋ̀:re?* 'it is crooked']	slim of krom	'sly or bad'
odossera [*o?túsera?* 'the fat']	speck	'bacon'
keye [*kʋ̀:ye* 'lard']	vet	'fat'
wistotcera [*owistóhsera?* 'butter']	smeer	'grease'
ostie [*óhstyʋ* 'bone']	been	'bone'
aghidawe [*aukí:ta?we?* 'I would sleep']	slaepen	'sleep'
sinekaty [*se?neká:ta?* 'your crotch area']	by slaepen	'(to have) intercourse'
Jankanque [*yakú:kwe* 'a woman']	heel moey	'very beautiful'
atsochwat [*katshókwas* 'I smoke']	Toback	'tobacco'

canonou [*kanv̀:nawv ʔ* 'tobacco pipe']	Tobacks pyp	'tobacco pipe'
esteronde [*waʔostarú:tiʔ* 'it started to rain']	reegen	'(to) rain'
waghideria [*wakaʔtarihv́:ʔv* 'I am perspiring']	sweeten	'(to) sweat'
kayontochke [*kahvtà:ke* 'on the meadow']	vlac saeylant	'flat, arable land'
ononda [*onú:taʔ* 'mountain']	Bergen	'mountain'
Cayanoghe [*kawehnò:ke* 'on the island']	eylanden	'islands'
schahohadee [*skaháhati* 'the other side of the road']	de over syede	'the reverse side'
caroo [*kà:ro* 'closer to me']	hier nae toe	'nearby'
cadadiiene [*katatyv́:ni* 'I am storing it for myself']	handelen	'(to) trade'
daweyate [*takatáweyaʔteʔ* 'I entered']	raet houden	'(to) hold council'
agotsioha	een kraeles arm	'a string of beads'
aquayanderen [*yukwayá:ner* 'we are chiefs']	een oversten	'a chief'
seronquatse [*shrukwehtáksvʔ* 'a really evil person']	een schellem	'a scoundrel'
sariwacksi [*serihwáksvʔ* 'your ways are bad']	een kakelaer	'a blasphemer'

onewachten [*ronowúhtu* 'he has told lies']	een logenaer	'a liar'
tenon commeyon [*tonvkú:yu?* 'how much shall I give you?']	wat wilt ghy hebben	'what do you want'
sinachkoo [*hatsináhkv* 'exorcist'][16]	duyvel jaegen	'(to) exorcise the devil'
adenocquat [*vhatenúhkwa?te?* 'he will give medicine']	medecyn salven	'(to) make medicine'
coenhaseren [*kuhnhà:sere?* 'I am here to heal you']^[17]	gesont maecken	'(to) heal'
sategat [*saté:ka?t* 'light the fire!']	lecht hout aen vier	'(to) ignite wood'
judicha [*yotékha?* 'it is burning']	het brandt	'conflagration'
catteges issewe [*kátke tutésewe?* 'when will you all come back']	wanneer comt ghy weer	'when shall you return'
tesenochte [*tvhsanúhtu?* 'do as you like']	ick weet het niet	'I do not know'
tegenhondi [*tvyokvhnhú:ti* 'the season when everything opens up']	int voor jaer	'in the spring'
otteyage	den soomer	'the summer'
augustuske [*vkewístoske?* 'I shall get cold']	den winter	'the winter'
katkaste [*katkátstus* 'I make soup']	eeten kooken	'(to) cook food'
jori [*yó:ri* 'it is cooked']	het is gaer	'it is cooked'
dequoquoha [*tewakóha* 'let's go and get it!']	wt jaegen gaen	'to go out hunting'

osqucha [*vhskóha⁷* 'you will get it']	ick salt haelen		'I shall fetch it'
seyendereii [*seyvterì:⁷u* 'you recognize the person']	ick kan hen wel		'I know them well'

kristoni asseroni
  [*keristú:ni* 'I am a metal-maker']
  [*o⁷serú:ni* 'axe-maker, European, French'][18]
	Nederlanders duytsen		'Dutch'

aderondackx [*atirú:taks* 'Algonquin Indians', 'Ojibway Indians'][19]	fransen of engelsen		'French or English'
anesagghena [*ronatshá:kanv* 'Eastern Algonquians'][20]	Mahikanders		'Mahikanders'
torsas [*othorè:ke* 'north']	omde nooert		'to the north'
Kanonnewage [*kanú:no wà:ke⁷* 'I go to New York City (Manhattan)']	de manhatas		'the Manhatas (Manhattan)'
onscat [*úska*]	1	Een	'one'
tiggeni [*tékeni*]	2	Twee	'two'
asse [*áhsv*]	3	dree	'three'
cayere [*kayé:ri*]	4	vier	'four'
wisck [*wisk*]	5	vyef	'five'
jayack [*yà:ya⁷k*]	6	ses	'six'
tsadack [*tsyá:ta*]	7	seeven	'seven'
hategon [*sha⁷té:ku*]	8	Acht	'eight'

tyochte	9	neegen	'nine'
[*tyóhtu*]			
oyere	10	Tien	'ten'
[*oyé:ri*]			
tawasse	40	veertich	'forty'
[*tewáhsv* '20']			
onscatteneyawe	100	hondert	'one-
[*vskatewvᵖnyáweᵖ*]			hundred'

NOTES

1. Van den Bogaert asked, or possibly gestured, to learn the word for a tool being used to scrape a deer hide. Through an obvious misunderstanding, he was provided the word for the hide being scraped.

2. The modern Mohawk word for deer is *oskenú:tu*. However, there is good reason to believe that Van den Bogaert actually heard the word *aque*, which must have been in use among the Mohawks at the time. Cognates of *aque* are found in Tuscarora, *a:kweh*, in the now extinct Susquehannock language, *Haagw*, and in Cherokee, *ahwi*. All of these terms are traceable to proto-Iroquoian (Mithun 1984, p. 265).

3. Van den Bogaert was unsure what to call an animal which did not occur in Europe. However, since a raccoon apparently looked to him like an exotic cat, he settled on the word 'cat'.

4. In modern Mohawk there is an animal term which fits exactly Van den Bogaert's entry for ox. This is *ukwetá:ku*, but it means 'squirrel'.

5. This is another case where Van den Bogaert recorded a term which has since disappeared from the Mohawk language. In modern Mohawk 'fox' is *tsítshoᵖ*. Old Huron had the term *tsinantonouq* 'grey fox', a cognate of Van den Bogaert's *senadondo* (Sagard 1968, p. 222).

6. The modern Mohawk term for 'marten' is *onú:koteᵖ*. It is conceivable that Van den Bogaert had heard and recorded the word *seranda* from a member of the Onondaga delegation while he was at the Oneida village. In a seventeenth-century French-Onondaga dictionary, marten (*martre*) is listed as *tcherannoha*, which could be a cognate of Van den Bogaert's *seranda* (Shea 1860, p. 69).

7. Van den Bogaert heard a term which is no longer used by

Mohawk speakers. In modern Mohawk 'crane' is *tehkáhu*. Old Huron *taron* 'duck' (Sagard 1968, p. 221) is a cognate of *tali* 'cranes'.

8. The modern Mohawk word for 'old woman' is *akokstóha*. Laurentian, another northern Iroquoian language which was recorded by the French explorer Jaques Cartier in 1535–1536, and is now extinct, had the term *Aggouette* 'women', which could be cognate to Van den Bogaert's *odasqueta* (cf. Biggar 1924, p. 242).

9. Perhaps the Mohawks wanted to express the idea that a woman in labor requires "support" or "a support".

10. In the Iroquois kinship system, a male parallel first cousin would be recognized by other parallel first cousins as a sibling, either an older or younger brother, or in the case of females, a younger or older sister.

11. *Canderes* could not be identified by Mohawk informants; however, old Onondaga has *ganneris* 'man's genitals' (Zeisberger 1887, p. 82).

12. Rather than learning the name of the fish he was pointing to or gesturing at, Van den Bogaert was provided their disposition.

13. This is an excellent example of the difficulties one can encounter in attempting to elicit responses regarding language concepts.

14. Compare *Ogwentsera 'peinture rouge'* (Bruyas 1863, p. 52).

15. The inquiry here was directed at learning what the word for rope was. Instead, the Indian questioned referred to the rope's strength, its quality.

16. See journal note 72.

17. Another equivalent in modern Mohawk may be *kuyunhahserú:ni* 'I make you healthy again'.

18. *Asseroni* 'axe-makers' is a reference to any European. On Canadian reserves it applies in particular to the French. The Mohawk name for the English became *tyorhvʔshá:kaʔ*, which means 'daylighters' or 'easterners', or simply, 'orientals.'

19. The *Aderondackx* or *Adirondacks* were the Algonkins (cf. Colden 1747, p. xiii). Lafitau (1977, p. 62) wrote that "the Iroquois give the Algonquin the name of *Rontaks*, that is to say, *Tree Eaters*."

20. The *Anesaggena*, the Mahicanders, were mentioned again in the 1640s by the Dutch clergyman Johannes Megapolensis, who referred to them as *Mahakans*, "otherwise called *Agotzagena*" (Jameson 1909, p. 172). Thirty years later, *Mahingans* is found in the dictionary of Father Bruyas (1863, p. 28), who also knew them under the name *ratsagannha*. He translated *Atsagannen* as *"parler une langue etrangere"*

(Bruyas 1863, p. 42). *Ratsagannha* and comparable forms were later applied to other Algonquian-speaking groups living east and southeast of the Mohawks. In 1780, Zeisberger wrote that "the Five Nations call the Mahicans, Delawares and all New England Savages 'Agozhaganta'" (Wheeler-Voegelin 1959, p. 45; cf. Brasser 1978b).

Bibliography

Abler, Thomas S.
1970   Longhouse and Palisade: Northeastern Iroquoian Villages of the Seventeenth Century. *Ontario History* 62:17–40.

Adney, Edwin T., and Chapelle, Howard I.
1964   *The Bark Canoes and Skin Boats of North America*: Washington, D.C.: The Smithsonian Institution.

Axtell, James, and Sturtevant, William C.
1980   The Unkindest Cut, or Who Invented Scalping? *William and Mary Quarterly* 37 (3):451–72.

Bartram, John.
1973   *A Journey from Pennsylvania to Onondaga in 1743*. Barre, Massachusetts: Imprint Society Inc.

Beauchamp, William M.
1895   Indian Nations of the Great Lakes. *American Antiquarian and Oriental Journal* 17:321–25.
1900   Aboriginal Occupation of New York. *New York State Museum Bulletin* 32. Albany.
1901   Wampum and Shell Articles Used by the New York Indians. *New York State Museum Bulletin* 41:319–480. Albany.
1905   Aboriginal Use of Wood in New York. *New York State Museum Bulletin* 89:87–272. Albany.
1907   Aboriginal Place Names of New York. *New York State Museum Bulletin 108, Archaeology* 12. Albany.

Benson, Adolph B., ed.
    1966   *Peter Kalm's Travels in North America: The English Version of 1770.* 2 vols. New York: Dover Publications.

Bigger, Henry P., ed.
    1924   The Voyages of Jacques Cartier: Published from the Originals with Translations, Notes and Appendices. *Publications of the Public Archives of Canada* 11. Ottawa.

Blau, Harold; Campisi, Jack; and Tooker, Elisabeth.
    1978   Onondaga. In *Handbook of North American Indians, the Northeast*, vol. 15. B. G. Trigger, ed., pp. 491–99. Washington, D.C.: The Smithsonian Institution.

Bradley, James W.
    1979   The Onondaga Iroquois: 1500–1655, A Study in Acculturative Change and Its Consequences. Ph.D. dissertation, Syracuse University.

Brasser, Ted J.
    1978a   Early Indian-European Contacts. In *Handbook of North American Indians, the Northeast*, vol. 15. B. G. Trigger, ed., pp. 78–88. Washington, D.C.: The Smithsonian Institution.
    1978b   Mahican. In *Handbook of North American Indians, the Northeast*, vol. 15. B. G. Trigger, ed., pp. 198–212. Washington, D.C.: The Smithsonian Institution.

Bruyas, Jacques.
    1863   Radical Words of the Mohawk Language, with their Derivatives. In Shea's Library of American Linguistics 10. New York: Cramoisy Press.

Calisch, I. M.
    1875   *Nederlandsch-Engelsch En Engelsch-Nederlandsch Woordenboek.* Netherlands: Tiel.

Campisi, Jack.
    1978   Oneida. In *Handbook of North American Indians, the Northeast*, vol. 15. B. G. Trigger, ed., pp. 481–90. Washington, D.C.: The Smithsonian Institution.

Carse, Mary.
    1949   The Mohawk Iroquois. *Archaeological Society of Connecticut Bulletin* 23:3–53.

Ceci, Lynn.
  1977   The Effect of European Contact and Trade on the Set-
           tlement Patterns of Indians in Coastal New York, 1524–
           1665. Ph.D. dissertation, The City University of New
           York.
  1982   The Value of Wampum among the New York Iroquois:
           A Case Study in Artifact Analysis. *Journal of Anthropol-*
           ogical Research 38 (1):97–107.

Champlain, Samuel de.
  1967   *Voyages of Samuel de Champlain, 1604–1618.* W. L. Grant,
           ed. Reprint. New York: Barnes and Noble.

Clarke, T. Wood.
  1940   *The Bloody Mohawk.* New York: MacMillan.

Colden, Cadwallader.
  1747   *The History of the Five Indian Nations Depending on the Prov-*
           ince of New-York in America [1958]. Ithaca, New York:
           Cornell University Press.

Cuoq, Jean-André.
  1882   *Lexique de la langue iroquoise avec notes et appendices.* Mon-
           treal: J. Chapleau.

Dineen, Robert.
  1975   Geology and Land Uses in the Pine Bush, Albany County,
           New York. *New York State Museum and Science Service,*
           Circular 47. Albany.

Dobyns, Henry F.
  1983   *Their Number Become Thinned: Native American Population*
           Dynamics in Eastern North America. Knoxville: University
           of Tennessee Press.

Engelbrecht, William.
  1972   The Reflection of Patterned Behavior in Iroquois Pottery
           Decoration. *Pennsylvania Archaeologist* 42 (3):1–15.

Feister, Lois M.
  1978   Linguistic Communication Between Dutch and Indians
           in New Netherland. In *Neighbors and Intruders: An Ethno-*
           Historical Exploration of the Indians of Hudson's River. L. M.
           Hauptman and J. Campisi, eds., pp. 181–96. *National*
           Museum of Man, Mercury Series 39. Ottawa.

Fenneman, N. M.
    1938   Physiography of Eastern United States. New York: McGraw-Hill.

Fenton, William N.
    1941   Masked Medicine Societies of the Iroquois. *Annual Report of the Smithsonian Institution for 1940*, pp. 397–430. Washington, D.C.
    1942a   Contacts Between Iroquois Herbalism and Colonial Medicine. *Annual Report of the Smithsonian Institution for 1941*, pp. 503–26. Washington, D.C.
    1942b   Songs from the Iroquois Longhouse: Program Notes for an Album of American Indian Music from the Eastern Woodlands. Washington, D.C.: The Smithsonian Institution.
    1950   The Roll Call of the Iroquois Chiefs: A Study of a Mnemonic Cane from the Six Nations Reserve. *Smithsonian Miscellaneous Collections* 111 (15):1–73. Washington, D.C.
    1971   The New York State Wampum Collection: The Case for the Integrity of Cultural Treasures. *Proceedings of the American Philosophical Society* 115 (6):437–61. Philadelphia.
    1978   Northern Iroquoian Culture Patterns. In *Handbook of North American Indians, the Northeast*, vol. 15. B. G. Trigger, ed., pp. 296–321. Washington, D.C.: The Smithsonian Institution.
    1987   *The False Faces of the Iroquois*. Norman: University of Oklahoma Press.

Fenton, William N., and Dodge, Ernest S.
    1949   An Elm Bark Canoe in the Peabody Museum of Salem. *American Neptune* 9 (3):185–206.

Fenton, William N., and Tooker, Elisabeth.
    1978   Mohawk. In *Handbook of North American Indians, the Northeast*, vol. 15. B. G. Trigger, ed., pp. 466–80. Washington, D.C.: The Smithsonian Institution.

Frey, Samuel L.
    1898   Notes on Arendt van Corlear's Journal of 1634. *Oneida Historical Society Transactions* 8:42–48.
    n.d.   Frey Papers. Box 9829, Folder 337. New York State Archives. Albany.

Gehring, Charles T., and Starna, William A.
1984 A Case of Fraud: The Dela Croix Letter and Map of 1634. *New York History* 66 (3):249–61.

Gramly, Richard M.
1977 Deerskins and Hunting Territories: Competition for a Scarce Resource of the Northeastern Woodlands. *American Antiquity* 42 (4):601–05

Grassmann, Thomas.
1969 *The Mohawk Indians and Their Valley*. Schenectady, New York: Hugo.

Grayson, Donald K.
1974 The Riverhaven No. 2 Vertebrate Fauna: Comments on Methods in Faunal Analysis and on Aspects of the Subsistence Potential of Prehistoric New York. *Man in the Northeast* 8:23–40.

Greene, Nelson, ed.
1925 *History of the Mohawk Valley*. 4 vols. Chicago: S. J. Clarke.

Hamell, George R.
1981 Through the Great Black Door: Transformation at the Threshhold. Paper Presented at the 1981 Conference on Iroquois Research, Institute on Man and Science, Rensselaerville, New York.

Heidenreich, Conrad E.
1971 *Huronia: A History and Geography of the Huron Indians, 1600–1650*. Toronto: McClelland and Stewart.

Herrick, James W.
1977 Iroquois Medical Botany. Ph.D. dissertation, State University of New York at Albany.

Hewitt, J. N. B.
1910 Seneca. In *Handbook of American Indians North of Mexico*. 2 vols. F. W. Hodge, ed., pp. 502–08. *Bureau of American Ethnology Bulletin* 30. Washington, D.C.

Hodge, Frederick W., ed.
1907– *Handbook of American Indians North of Mexico*. 2 vols. *Bu-*
1910 *reau of American Ethnology Bulletin* 30. Washington, D.C. (Reprinted: New York: Rowman and Littlefield, 1971.)

Huey, Paul R.
1975 History of the Pine Bush from 1624 to 1815, Albany

County, New York. *In* Geology and Land Uses in the Pine Bush, Albany County, New York, by R. Dineen, pp. 7–8. *New York State Museum and Science Service, Circular* 47. Albany.

Hunt, George T.
1940   *The Wars of the Iroquois: A Study in Intertribal Trade Relations.* Madison: University of Wisconsin Press.

Hutchinson, Holmes.
1834   Holmes Hutchinson Maps, vol. 9, Minden to Amsterdam. Series 848. New York State Archives. Albany.

Jameson, J. Franklin, ed.
1909   *Narratives of New Netherland.* New York: Charles Scribner's Sons.

Jennings, Francis.
1978   Susquehannock. In *Handbook of North American Indians, the Northeast*, vol. 15. B. G. Trigger, ed., pp. 362–67. Washington, D.C.: The Smithsonian Institution.

JR (Jesuit Relations).
1896–   The Jesuit Relations and Allied Documents. 73 vols. R.
1901   G. Thwaites, ed. New York: Pageant Book Company.

Kirkland, Samuel.
1980   *The Journals of Samuel Kirkland.* W. Pilkington, ed. Clinton, New York: Hamilton College.

Kluyver, A., ed.
1904   *Woordenboek der Nederlandsche Taal.* Vol. 9. The Hague. Netherlands.

Kurath, Gertrude P.
1964   Iroquois Music and Dance: Ceremonial Arts of Two Seneca Longhouses. *Bureau of American Ethnology Bulletin* 187:1–259. Washington, D.C.

Lafitau, Joseph-François.
1974,   *Customs of the American Indians Compared with the Customs*
1977   *of Primitive Times.* 2 vols. W. N. Fenton and E. L. Moore, eds. and trans. Toronto: The Champlain Society.

Lathers, William, and Sheehan, Edward J.
1937   The Iroquois Occupation in the Mohawk Valley. *Van Epps-Hartley Bulletin* 2 (1):5–9. Schenectady.

Lenig, Donald.
  1977   Of Dutchmen, Beaver Hats, and Iroquois. *In* Current
          Perspectives in Northeastern Archaeology: Essays in
          Honor of William A. Ritchie. R. E. Funk and C. F. Hayes
          III, eds., pp. 71–84. *New York State Archaeological Asso-
          ciation, Researches and Transactions* 17 (1). Rochester and
          Albany.

Megapolensis, Johannes, Jr.
  1909   A Short Account of the Mohawk Indians . . . 1644. In
          Narratives of New Netherland. J. Franklin Jameson, ed.,
          pp. 165–80. New York: Charles Scribner's Sons.

Mithun, Marianne.
  1984   The Proto-Iroquoians: Cultural Reconstruction from
          Lexical Materials. In *Extending the Rafters: Interdisciplinary
          Approaches to Iroquoian Studies.* M. K. Foster, J. Campisi,
          and M. Mithun, eds., pp. 269–81. Albany: State Uni-
          versity of New York Press.

Morgan, Lewis H.
  1881   Houses and House-Life of the American Aborigines.
          (Contributions to North American Ethnology 4). U.S.
          Geological and Geographical Survey of the Rocky Moun-
          tain Region. Washington, D.C.
  1962   League of the Iroquois. New York: Corinth Books.

O'Callaghan, Edmund B.
  1846   *History of New Netherland, or New York Under the Dutch*, vol.
          1. New York: D. Appleton and Company.
  1850   *Documentary History of the State of New York*, vol. 3. Albany:
          Weed, Parsons

Parker, Arthur C.
  1910   Iroquois Uses of Maize and Other Food Plants. *New York
          State Museum Bulletin* 144 (482):5–113. Albany.
  1923   *Seneca Myths and Folk Tales.* Buffalo: Buffalo Historical
          Society.
  1928   Indian Medicine and Medicine Men. *Archaeological Report
          of the Minister of Education, Annual Reports*, pp. 57–69.
          Toronto.

Pendergast, James F.
  1979   The Hochelaga Palisade. *Ottawa Archaeologist* 9 (3):8–18.

Pratt, Peter P.
    1976   Archaeology of the Oneida Iroquois. *Occasional Publications in Northeastern Archaeology*, vol. 1. George's Mill, New Hampshire.

Reid, William M.
    1901   *The Mohawk Valley, N.Y.: Its Legends and History.* New York: G. P. Putnam's Sons.

Reilly, Edgar M., Jr.
    1975   Biota. *In* Geology and Land Uses in the Pine Bush, Albany County, New York, by R. Dineen, pp. 9–10. *New York State Museum and Science Service, Circular* 47. Albany.

Ritchie, William A.
    1969   *The Archaeology of New York State*, (2d ed.) New York: Natural History Press.

Ritchie, William A., and Funk, Robert E.
    1973   Aboriginal Settlement Patterns in the Northeast. *New York State Museum and Science Service Memoir* 20. Albany.

Ruttenber, Edward M.
    1906   Indian Geographical Names in the Valley of Hudson's River, the Valley of the Mohawk and on the Delaware. *New York State Historical Association Proceedings* 6. Albany

Sagard, Gabriel.
    1968   *The Long Journey to the Country of the Hurons.* G. M. Wrong, ed. New York: Greenwood Press.

Sewell, Willem.
    1754   *Groot Woordenboek der Engelsche en Nederduytsche Taalen.* 5th ed. Amsterdam: Jacob Ter Beek.

Shea, John D. G., ed.
    1860   *A French-Onondaga Dictionary, from a Manuscript of the Seventeenth Century.* In Shea's Library of American Linguistics 1. New York: Cramoisy Press.

Shimony, Annemarie A.
    1961   Conservatism Among the Iroquois at the Six Nations Reserve. *Yale University Publications in Anthropology* 65. New Haven.

Snow, Dean R.
    1980   *The Archaeology of New England.* New York: Academic Press.

Snow, Dean R., and Starna, William A.

1980   A Preliminary Research Design for the Mohawk Valley Project. Paper presented at the 1980 Conference on Iroquois Research, Institute on Man and Science, Rensselaerville, New York.

1984   Sixteenth-Century Depopulation: A Preliminary Review from the Mohawk Valley. Paper presented at the Forty-Ninth Annual Meeting of the Society for American Archaeology, Portland, Oregon.

Speck, Frank G.

1945   The Iroquois: A Study in Cultural Evolution. *Cranbrook Institute of Science Bulletin* 23. Bloomfield Hills, Michigan.

Starna, William A.

1976   Late Archaic Lifeways in the Middle Mohawk Valley: A Framework for Further Study. Ph.D. dissertation, State University of New York at Albany.

1980   Mohawk Iroquois Populations: A Revision. *Ethnohistory* 27 (4):371–82.

Stokes, I. N. Phelps, ed.

1967   The Iconography of Manhattan Island, 1498–1909. New York: Arno Press.

Sykes, Clark S.

1980   Swidden Horticulture and Iroquoian Settlement. *Archaeology of Eastern North America* 8:45–52.

Tooker, Elisabeth.

1964   An Ethnology of the Huron Indians, 1615–1649. *Bureau of American Ethnology Bulletin* 190. Washington, D.C.

1978   The League of the Iroquois: Its History, Politics and Ritual. In *Handbook of North American Indians, the Northeast,* vol. 15. B. G. Trigger, ed., pp. 418–41. Washington, D.C.: The Smithsonian Institution.

1984   Women in Iroquois Society. In *Extending the Rafters: Interdisciplinary Approaches to Iroquoian Studies.* M. K. Foster, J. Campisi, M. Mithun, eds., pp. 109–123. Albany: State University of New York Press.

Trelease, Allen W.

1960   *Indian Affairs in Colonial New York: The Seventeenth Century.* Ithaca, New York: Cornell University Press.

Trigger, Bruce G.
 1969   *The Huron: Farmers of the North.* New York: Holt, Rinehart and Winston.
 1971   The Mohawk-Mahican War (1624–1628): The Establishment of a Pattern. *Canadian Historical Review* 52 (3):276–86.
 1976   *The Children of Aataentsic: A History of the Huron People to 1660.* 2 vols. Montreal: McGill-Queen's University Press.
 1978   Early Iroquoian Contacts with Europeans. In *Handbook of North American Indians, the Northeast,* vol. 15. B. G. Trigger, ed., pp. 344–56. Washington, D.C.: The Smithsonian Institution.
 1985   *Natives and Newcomers: Canada's Heroic Age Reconsidered.* Montreal: McGill-Queen's University Press.

Tuck, James A.
 1971   *Onondaga Iroquois Prehistory.* Syracuse, New York: Syracuse University Press.

Van der Donck, Adriaen.
 1968   *A Description of the New Netherlands.* T. F. O'Donnell, ed. Syracuse, New York: Syracuse University Press.

Van Laer, A. J. F., ed.
 1908   *Van Rensselaer Bowier Manuscripts.* Albany: University of the State of New York.
 1924   *Documents Relating to New Netherland, 1624–26.* San Marino, California: Henry E. Huntington Library.

Van Loon, L. G.
 1939–   Letter from Jeronimus de la Croix to the Commissary at
 1940   Fort Orange and a Hitherto Unknown Map Relating to Surgeon Van den Bogaert's Journey Into the Mohawk Country, 1634–1635. In *The Dutch Settlers Society Yearbook* XV, 1939–1940, pp. 1–9. Albany.

Waugh, Frederick W.
 1916   Iroquois Foods and Food Preparation. *Anthropological Series 12, Memoirs of the Canadian Geological Survey* 86. Ottawa.

Wheeler-Voegelin, Erminie.
 1959   Some Remarks and Annotations Concerning Indians in North America from Memoirs of Rev. David Zeisberger and Others. *Ethnohistory* 6 (1):42–69.

White, Marian E.
   1978a   Neutral and Wenro. In *Handbook of North American Indians, the Northeast*, vol. 15. B. G. Trigger, ed., pp. 407–411. Washington, D.C.: The Smithsonian Institution.
   1978b   Erie. In *Handbook of North American Indians, the Northeast*, vol. 15. B. G. Trigger, ed., pp. 412–17. Washington, D.C.: The Smithsonian Institution.
Wilson, General James Grant.
   1895   Corlear and His Journal of 1634. *The Independent* 47 (October 3, 1895), 1–4.
   1896   Arent Van Curler and His Journal of 1634–35. *American Historical Association Annual Report for 1895*. Pp. 81–101.
Wray, Charles F., and Schoff, Harry L.
   1953   A Preliminary Report on the Seneca Sequence in Western New York, 1550–1687. *Pennsylvania Archaeologist* 23 (2):53–63.
Wright, Benjamin.
   1811   An Examination of the Country for a Canal from Rome to Waterford on the North Side of the Mohawk River. Manuscript Collection. Erie Canal Museum Library. Syracuse, New York.
Zeisberger, David.
   1887   *Zeisberger's Indian Dictionary*. Cambridge, Mass.: John Wilson and Son.

A JOURNEY INTO MOHAWK AND ONEIDA COUNTRY, 1634–1635

was composed in 10 on 13 Baskerville on a Mergenthaler Linotron 202
by World Composition Services, Inc.;
printed by sheet-fed offset on 60-pound, acid-free Glatfelter Natural Hi Bulk,
Smyth-sewn and bound over binder's boards in Holliston Roxite C
by Braun-Brumfield, Inc.;
with dust jackets printed in 2 colors
by Braun-Brumfield, Inc.;
designed by Mary Peterson Moore;
and published by

SYRACUSE UNIVERSITY PRESS
SYRACUSE, NEW YORK 13244-5160